D1320218

LOU GEHRIG

The story of not only a great ball p
man who became a symbol of courage a
and kindness to millions who were not
in baseball. Lou Gehrig was not a drama
in the sense that Babe Ruth was dramatic,
career was a sustained drama from his boyh
the sidewalks and sandlots of New York to his
death at the age of thirty-eight.

For boys, for baseball fans, for the young in sp
of any age, this story of Lou Gehrig must prove a
unending source of inspiration.

LOU GEHRIG

A Quiet Hero

FRANK GRAHAM

G. P. PUTNAM'S SONS, NEW YORK

Designed by Robert Josephy

CONTENTS

1. The Boy at Wrigley Field 3
2. A Student at Commerce High 20
3. College Years 32
4. The Yankee Scout 50
5. Joining the Yankees 61
6. Batting Slump in Hartford 72
7. Spring Training in New Orleans 86
8. 1925—Lou Becomes a Regular 98
9. Ruth, Gehrig, and Meusel 110
10. The Death of Miller Huggins 124
11. The Coming of Joe McCarthy 137
12. Romance and Marriage 158
13. Lou Maintains His Record 165
14. The Shadows Lengthen 182
15. Retirement in 1939 196
16. The Hall of Fame 212
17. The Parole Board 231
18 The Last Days 245

Photographic Illustrations Will Be Found
Following Page 138

LOU GEHRIG

1. The Boy at Wrigley Field

ON a June day in 1920, at Wrigley Field, Lane Technical High School of Chicago was playing the High School of Commerce from New York in a game for the inter-city baseball championship. Lane scored four runs in the first inning, but the Commerce boys hammered back, and by the time the teams reached the ninth inning the score was tied at 8-8. Commerce filled the bases, and a wide-shouldered, thick-limbed kid stepped to the plate and hit the first ball pitched to him over the right-field fence.

After the game the Commerce coach beamed at the newspapermen who had rushed down to the dressing room.

"That was nothing," he said. "He hit a ball further than that out of Dexter Park in Brooklyn last week."

But it was something. It was a tremendous feat for a schoolboy to hit a ball out of a major league park, and that night for the first time the name of

Lou Gehrig went out over the wires that stretch across the country. One writer hailed him as the schoolboy Babe Ruth. And that was the first time Gehrig's name ever was coupled with that of the Babe.

The stories were read with interest by college baseball coaches, by major and minor league managers and scouts. From that day the boy's path was marked clearly. Three years later it was to lead him to the Yankee Stadium.

As the years unwound before him he followed that path to heights of which as a boy he could not have dreamed, and when death, in a swift race, overtook him on June 2, 1941, James M. Kahn was to write of him in the *New York Sun:*

"Lou Gehrig was the greatest ball player ever produced in New York. He was one of the greatest ball players ever produced anywhere. For years a teammate of Babe Ruth, he was many times nominated to become the Babe's successor. But he was nothing like Ruth. He did not have the Babe's booming Falstaffian personality, nor the Babe's capacity for capturing the imagination of the crowd and electrifying it.

4

"Gehrig was quiet, somewhat shy, and sincerely modest. He was conscientious, uncomplaining, and persevering. He was not a natural athlete and had to work laboriously to become a great ball player. So it was, too, with his popularity. He was not a natural crowd pleaser. But just as his consistently fine ball playing, day after day, wore down the opposition and steadily drove him upward to a place among the greatest players of all time, so did his fine qualities, his character and his courage in the face of adversity, earn him a place in the affections of the public. When he retired from baseball he did so with the esteem and the sympathy of the whole country."

Only thirty-eight years old when he died, Lou had had a crowded and exciting life. Millions had seen him smash out home runs or make dazzling plays at first base as he took part in the astounding total of 2,130 consecutive games. To other millions, although they never had seen him, he was a familiar figure because they had heard or read so much about him. His travels covered this country, Europe, and the Orient. His salary and his share of world-series gate receipts had yielded about $400,000. The by-products of his career—endorsements, syndicated articles under his signature, a motion picture in which he was starred, radio broadcasts—had netted him another $100,000.

Fame and wealth touched him lightly and could not mar his simplicity nor the virtues with which he was endowed. When death claimed him he had become a symbol of decency and kindliness and courage, and this surprised him because he had not meant to become a symbol and never could quite understand the regard in which he was held not only by baseball fans but also by those who would not go across the street to see a ball game.

The child of Henry and Christina Gehrig, natives of Germany—there had been one child in the family before him and two came after him, but they died in infancy and he had no recollection of them—he was born at 1994 Second Avenue, near 102nd Street, on June 19, 1903, and was christened Henry Louis. When he was a small boy his parents, after several preliminary moves, settled at 170th Street and Amsterdam Avenue, and there, within sight and sound of the park where the New York American League team, known then as the Highlanders, first played, he grew up, attended elementary school, and learned to play baseball, football, and soccer on corner lots.

The neighborhood has changed greatly in recent years. Where the Highlanders played, the tall buildings of the Medical Center stand. Apartment houses, row on row and block on block, have crowded out the sandlots. But in those days there was room for a boy to play, and Lou played tirelessly at his games. Baseball from the first spring thaw to the first turning of the leaves. Then football and soccer.

"The boy must grow big and strong," his father said.

"And he must have an education," his mother said.

"Yes, an education. He must work hard and study and learn to be . . . what, Lou? What would you like to be?"

"An engineer," the boy said.

"An engineer? What kind of engineer?"

"I don't know. . . . An engineer. I want to build bridges and things."

His father nodded.

"Yes," he said. "Yes, an engineer."

"Then you must study, Lou," his mother said. "You must go to high school and to college."

"But he must play, too," his father said. "He must be strong."

7

His father belonged to a *Turnverein,* and there he took Lou, and the boy was fascinated by the parallel bars, the horses, the rings, the pulleys, the weights, the wrestling mats. On winter afternoons he exercised there and soon became one of the best of the younger gymnasts. He had found something to do between the end of the football season and the coming of spring. His young body was being hardened and developed.

Meanwhile, things were going badly at home. His father, worn by years of toil as a wrought iron worker, had become virtually an invalid. He could not work for more than a few days at a time. There were weeks, even months, when he couldn't work at all. Lou wanted to leave school and go to work, but his mother wouldn't hear of it.

"No," she said. "You must have a college education."

And so she assumed the burden of support for the family. She cooked, sewed, cleaned, became caretaker of the house in which they lived. Lou helped her in the morning before going to school, helped her again in the evening before doing his lessons. She was frugal and wise and spent her small income carefully, so that if they had few luxuries, they always managed to have plenty of plain but nourishing food.

One of the boy's favorite dishes was pickled eels—pickled by his mother. In later years when baseball writers asked him what was the source of his power as a hitter, he would laugh and say:

"Pickled eels!"

And once when the whole Yankee team was in a hitting slump, he arrived at the clubhouse with six jars of pickled eels from his mother's shelves. He was half in jest, half in earnest, as he insisted that all the players eat some of them just before the game. Pickled eels had become almost a superstition with him, and his faith in their efficacy was heightened when the Yankees emerged from their slump that afternoon and clouted an unhappy White Sox pitcher out of the box.

Clothing was no problem to him in the lean days of his youth. All he needed was underwear, socks, shirt, coat, a pair of pants, and stout shoes. In the summer he discarded the coat. He never wore a vest, an overcoat, or a hat. His mother, naturally concerned about his appearance, often wished aloud that she could afford more and better clothing for him. but he would laugh and say:

"What's the matter with me? I look all right, don't I?"

He asked for little, was content with what he had, and was worried only over his father's condition and the fact that his mother had to work to support him.

"Never mind," he used to say. "I'll get a job one of these days, and then you can quit work and we can have the best doctors in New York for Pop."

He had entered the High School of Commerce down on Sixty-fifth Street, just off Columbus Avenue, when his mother and father obtained employment in the Sigma Nu fraternity house at Columbia University, his mother as cook, his father as handy man.

The new job meant long hours for Lou and his mother and father. They would get up early in the morning and ride down to the house on the Amsterdam Avenue car. Lou would help to prepare breakfast and then go on down to school. In the evening, he would return to the house, wait on table, clear it when dinner was over, and then help to wash and dry the dishes. Then they would go home to bed. His studies were becoming increasingly difficult for him, since he was not a brilliant student but must work hard at them. He would do his homework at the fraternity house or on the street cars.

He was popular with the fraternity members. "The Little Dutch Boy," they called him. They discovered that he not only liked to play ball but played it very well. On spring evenings, when his mother could spare him, they invited him to play with them on South Field. A few years later he was to star on that field both as a baseball and a football player. One day he was to drive a ball out of the field and across 116th Street, where it struck on the steps of the library.

But that was ahead of him. Now he was a student at Commerce and, between and after classes, one of the school's outstanding athletes. He wasn't the best player on the baseball team—that distinction was had by Bunny Bonura, the short stop—but he was the most versatile, pitching, playing first base and the outfield, and he was the best and most powerful hitter on the team. He was the fullback on the football team, played on the soccer and basketball teams, and could outdo the other boys in the gymnasium.

On a fall day in 1920 he twice humbled Commercial High School of Brooklyn on Commercial Field. In the morning he kicked the decisive goal in a soccer game, and in the afternoon he threw a 40-yard forward pass for the touchdown that won the game for Commerce, 9 to 6.

"He was the greatest athlete I ever coached," Harry Kane was to say years afterward. "He was almost as big then as he was when he was at the height of his career with the Yankees, and he had the same team spirit and eagerness to win. It was a pleasure to coach him, for he constantly wanted to learn and improve his play, and when a weakness cropped up in his play he worked at it until he had eradicated it.

"For instance, when I first saw him, which was in his junior year, and I had him in both baseball and football, his main weakness in baseball was his inability to hit left-handed curve ball pitching. We set to work together, and after a few weeks of practice, day in and day out, he completely overcame his fault."

The lot back of the school was too small for use as a practice field. The home grounds were at the Catholic Protectory, away up in the east Bronx, and the team practiced there or in Central Park. It was a long and tedious journey from the school to the Protectory, for in those days the transportation facilities were not as adequate as they are now. But the boys didn't complain. The trip complicated Gehrig's daily routine because, of course, he had to come all the way back to the Sigma Nu house when the practice or the game was over.

12

One day, when a game was dragging into extra innings, he obviously was fretful, and Kane said:

"Don't worry. We'll get them."

"I know we will," Lou said. "I'm not worried about that. I'm worried because I'll be late and won't be able to help my mother with the dinner."

"That was the only time I ever heard him complain," Kane said. "But he wasn't worried long. He broke up the game in the next inning."

The trip to Chicago for the game with Lane Tech was the greatest adventure the boys on the Commerce team ever had had. Few of them had been as much as a hundred miles from New York. Lou, for one, never had been west of Newark or north of Poughkeepsie.

When the boys first heard they had been selected to play this game, they crowded about Kane, hammering him with questions, for Kane had seen a good deal of the world, on his own and as a soldier in France during the World War, and they assumed he knew all the answers. As a matter of fact, he knew most of them. But nobody could know the answers to all the questions that boys could ask in a spot like that.

13

Harry did his best. He told them what it was like to sleep in a Pullman and eat in a dining car. And how they must be careful to look after their luggage and what they should take with them. The last was no problem to most of the boys. Least of all was it a problem to Lou. But when the great day came, Mrs. Gehrig packed his little bag for him—toothbrush, comb and brush, underwear, socks, and shirts.

Several hundred boys were at the Grand Central to see the team off. And it was just a team. Nine kids, with their coach. The rooters were very enthusiastic.

"Knock 'em off!" they were yelling. "Hey, Lou, when you go to bat, show 'em where you live!"

"Good luck, Al!"

"Give 'em that old fast ball, Eli!"

"Show 'em how, Bunny! Show 'em how!"

At last, as the shouts died away behind them, the train moved slowly out of the station and the kids sat there in their car looking at each other, scarcely believing they actually were on their way to Chicago: Eli Jacobs, the pitcher; Al McLaughlin, the catcher; Gehrig, the first-baseman; Al Rosamondo, the second-baseman; Bunny Bonura, the short stop; Sewell Johnson, the third-baseman; and the outfielders, Schacht (a brother of Al Schacht, former pitcher and now

14

nationally famous as a baseball clown), Stark, and Sammy Strum.

The first phase of the great adventure, after the exciting departure and the feel of the wheels turning under the train, was dinner in the dining car. That evening before they retired there were two more thrills. Word that the team was aboard had spread through the train, and the boys had two visitors, distinguished in two widely separated fields: William Howard Taft, former President of the United States and at the time Justice of the Supreme Court; and Joe Frisco, the stuttering comedian.

Justice Taft joked with the boys, told them numerous experiences he had had in and out of office and in his wide travels and, before bidding them good night, wished them luck in their game. And then Frisco came in and had them rolling in the aisles with his gags and comic soft-shoe dances.

Then came the final adventure of the day—going to bed in Pullman berths, and lying there in the dark as the train rushed through the night, its whistle screeching as it approached a grade crossing or a station.

Wonder if Lou, lying in his berth, unable to sleep at first because of the excitement that had been

15

crowded into the last few hours, looked ahead and saw, somehow, the endless miles he was destined to travel in Pullman cars, up and down and across the country?

When they reached Chicago, there was the further excitement of going to a hotel and being conducted to their rooms—two boys to a room—and then a sightseeing tour of the great city on Lake Michigan. The boys looked upon the lake unbelieving. A lake, to them, had been a small body of water such as they had seen in Central Park or on some summer journey to Long Island or New Jersey or the Catskills. This— why this looked like the ocean.

And then the ball game.

"I never thought we'd win it, the way it began," Harry Kane has said. "We couldn't score in the first inning, and when they went to bat, I thought the game had broken wide open. Eli Jacobs, really a fine schoolboy pitcher, must have had stage fright and was wild, and then when he did manage to get the ball over the plate he didn't have his usual stuff on it and they hit it hard. To make matters worse, McLaughlin, running back for a foul fly, wrenched his left ankle badly. Lane got four runs and there we were—four runs behind in the first inning, our

16

pitcher staggering all over the box and our catcher so lame he hardly could walk.

"I should have taken both Jacobs and McLaughlin out of the game, but I couldn't. We had only the nine players with us. So there was nothing to do but keep them in there. McLaughlin became so lame as the innings went on that I almost had to carry him up to the plate and back at the start of their half of an inning or when it was his turn to bat. But he was a dead game kid and hung in there and did the best he could and was valuable because he kept the whole team on its toes. Meanwhile, Jacobs had settled down and was pitching good ball, although Lane tagged him for four more runs—one at a time—between the first inning and the eighth. And then we started to hit, and by the end of the eighth we had them tied at 8-8, and now I knew we were going to win.

"You may not believe me, but I really knew in my heart what was going to happen when we started to hit in the ninth—and got the bases filled—and Gehrig walked up to the plate. He had played a great game and made a couple of hits before that, and he always was a great kid in a pinch, and I would have bet my life he was going to slough one this time.

"'Go and hit one out of the park!' I said to him.

17

"It was almost an order, I felt so confident he could do it. When he did—and what a wallop that was—our kids went crazy—and I don't believe I was exactly sane at the moment.

"Of course, we still had to get them out in their half of the inning. But that was easy. They were licked and they knew it, and we were so high we could have got anybody out. One-two-three—bing! The ball game was over."

The reception the Commerce players received when they returned to New York surpassed anything a schoolboy team ever had experienced in the big town. Gehrig, of course, was the main hero, and the rooters at the station—practically the entire student body—carried him from the gate to the exit, where cabs awaited them. They were driven to the school, where classes had been suspended for the morning, and there was an uproarious demonstration in the auditorium.

It was Lou's first brush with fame that extended beyond the confines of the New York high school circuit. He had heard a crowd, even though it had come to cheer for the opposing team, roar for him in Chicago. His name had been flashed over the wires from one end of the country to the other and had appeared in countless newspapers, from the great metropolitan dailies to the papers in the smallest towns reached by the press associations' wires. His name had been linked, however lightly, with Babe Ruth, the new home run king who had come to New York from Boston that year and was thrilling crowds at the Polo Grounds and wherever the Yankees played.

The narrow circumstances to which he had been born and in which he had lived were beginning to break and fall about him. He was emerging from the obscurity which he had accepted as his fate.

He was excited, naturally. But the modesty and the firmness of character that had been bred into him and nurtured by his parents kept him on a level keel. So he could return, the next day, to his studies and to the chores he did to help his mother and father to make a living for all of them and keep their little home together.

2. A Student at Commerce High

THE head of the house at Sigma Nu—head of the table, the young man was called—was Robert W. Watt, distinguished both as a student and as a ball player on the varsity team. He was later to play with the Detroit Tigers for a time and then to retire and, eventually, to become a businessman in New York. Meanwhile, he was to help in fashioning the life of Lou Gehrig.

It was Bobby Watt who had hired the Gehrigs, and he first saw Lou as a husky kid helping his mother in the kitchen or running errands for the fraternity brothers. He grew to be very fond of the little family—and then the nation entered the World War and Bobby was off to France with the troops and the Gehrigs were lost in the swirl that the war had produced.

In 1919, Bobby returned to Columbia, this time

as Graduate Manager of Athletics, and plunged enthusiastically into his new job. He had to make up the schedules for all the teams, supervise the work of the coaches, attend to the thousand and one details that are the lot of the graduate manager at a university of the size and importance of Columbia.

In the early fall of 1920, a request came to his desk. It was made jointly by the High School of Commerce and its chief rival in sports, De Witt Clinton. Object, the playing of the annual football game on South Field. Bobby was inclined to grant it, but since it was a special matter, beyond the range of his regular duties, he had to take it up with the Athletic Council.

"No," the council said, practically as one man.

"But why?"

"You know what these high-school boys are like," one testy member said. "The game will be followed by a riot, I am sure."

Bobby smiled.

"You mean the kids will be excited and will be punching each other and possibly tearing down the goal posts?"

"Exactly."

"Well," Bobby said, "it seems to me that from time to time I've seen our kids do the same thing. But they never tore down any of the buildings around the field or even broke any windows. And since these kids are smaller than ours, I don't think the campus will be in danger of utter destruction. . . . Besides, getting really serious about it, I think it would be a nice gesture on our part and would indicate that we have some interest in the local high schools. After all, we want the best students we can get from the local schools, and I don't think it is a bad idea to plant Columbia in their minds."

The members of the council looked at each other. They hadn't considered that angle at all.

"I think Mr. Watt is right," one of them said. "I'm in favor of permitting the game."

The others nodded assent. And so the game was scheduled.

The day it was played, Bobby Watt and Frank (Buck) O'Neill, now an insurance man in New York and then but recently brought down from Syracuse, where he had been very successful, to coach the Columbia football team, were seated high in the bleachers. It was a thrilling game, and the outstanding player in it was a broad-shouldered, thick-legged kid in the Commerce backfield. This kid ran hard, passed accurately, and sent long, booming punts down the field.

O'Neill's eyes popped.

"What's his name?" he asked.

Bobby consulted his program.

"Gehrig," he said.

"Know anything about him?"

"Not a thing."

He was sincere. The war, his return to this country, the press of work during the last year and a half, the new interests that had come into his life—these had swept away his memories of the Gehrig family, and not for an instant did he connect this young giant, ripping and tearing on the field, with the smiling, silent "Little Dutch Boy" of the Sigma Nu house.

"I'd like to find out something about him," Buck said. "I'd like to have a football player like that."

"Well," Bobby said, "we'll look him up after the game—find out how he stands scholastically and whether he would be interested in coming here."

The game over, they climbed down from the bleachers and started for the dressing rooms in the basement of Furnald Hall. The crowd was surging across the field, the Commerce kids cheering their heroes, jeering at the beaten foe. Out of the crowd a man rushed at Watt and O'Neill.

"Why, Mr. Gehrig!" Bobby said. "How are you?"

"Hello, Mr. Watt!" he cried.

23

Mr. Gehrig was so excited he could scarcely talk.

"Fine! Fine!" he said. "Fine!"

"And Mrs. Gehrig?"

"Fine! Fine! What do you think of Louie?"

"Louie? Oh, yes. The little boy. What do I think of him? Why—"

"That's Louie!" Mr. Gehrig said.

He pointed to where Gehrig, laughing, was struggling in the grip of his hysterical admirers.

"That's Louie. What do you think of him?"

"That's your boy? Louie? The boy I used to know at the house?"

"Sure! Sure! But a big boy now. A good football player, eh, Mr. Watt?"

Bobby looked at O'Neill, who was grinning widely.

"I should say he is, Mr. Gehrig," Bobby said. "By the way, what class is he in?"

"He graduates in February."

"My, my. It doesn't seem possible. Little Louie about to graduate! Is he going to college?"

"Oh, yes. By all means."

"Has he made up his mind where he is going?"

"Twenty offers he has, Mr. Watt! Twenty! Twenty-four! Look. I have some of them here."

He pulled some letters from his pocket.

"Look!"

Bobby looked. So did O'Neill. O'Neill wasn't grinning now.

"Let's go over and talk to him," Bobby said. "Come with us, Mr. Gehrig."

They crossed the field, passed the guards, and went down the steps of Furnald Hall. Lou was getting out of his uniform. He looked up.

"Why, Mr. Watt!" he said. "Gosh, I'm glad to see you."

"I'm glad to see you, too, Lou," Bobby said. "Lou, this is Mr. O'Neill, our football coach."

"How do you do, sir."

"I'm glad to meet you, Lou. You're quite a football player."

"Thank you, sir."

"You'll soon be ready for college, eh, Lou?" Bobby asked.

"Yes, sir."

"Made up your mind where you will go?"

"No, sir. Not yet."

"He has twenty-four offers," Mr. Gehrig said proudly.

"Yes," Bobby said. "That's great, Lou."

He turned to Mr. Gehrig.

"Do you suppose Mrs. Gehrig would drop in and see me at my office tomorrow?" he asked. "I'd like very much to see her. There are some things I want to talk to her about."

"Why, certainly," Mr. Gehrig said. "She will be glad to. We often have spoken of you."

"That's fine," Bobby said.

He and O'Neill left the boy with his father and went up the steps to the field.

"So you think you'd like to have him, eh, Buck?" he asked.

"I should say I would," O'Neill said. "What a football player! What a build!"

"Well," Bobby said, thoughtfully, "with luck we may get him. . . . I hope he has sufficient credits."

The next day Mrs. Gehrig was at the office.

"Lou is getting ready to go to college," Bobby said.

"Yes."

"Have you any idea where you would like him to go?"

"I don't know. I have thought it over a great deal, but I can't make up my mind. He doesn't seem to know, either. First it is this one, then that one. And it isn't making it any easier for him because so many of them want him."

26

"Do you want him to go away to college?"

She was silent for a moment.

"No," she said slowly. "No, I do not. But I realize that he is growing up, and if he wants to go away I do not want to . . . to . . . prevent him."

"Well," Bob said, "why not send him here? He could live at home, just as he always has. If he needed any help or advice, I would always be here for him to call upon. And as far as the educational advantages are concerned, I don't know where he could go to find better."

Mrs. Gehrig's face brightened.

"Yes!" she said. "To Columbia! I am sure he would like to come here. I will talk to him tonight."

And so, ultimately, it was arranged that Lou should go to Columbia.

"I didn't know until later that he was a baseball player," Bobby Watt said, recently. "We were interested in him only as a football player."

There came the closing days of his years at Commerce. The last friendly scuffle in the little back lot. The last pushing and shoving in the lunch room at the noon hour, the last ball game. And then Commencement and the Principal giving out the diplomas in the auditorium, packed with the proud mothers and fathers of the boys in the graduating class. The names of the graduates being called and each stepping up to get his diploma and the crowd applauding. And then the name:

"Henry Louis Gehrig!"

Applause, a little louder for him than for many of the other boys. For he was an athlete. A football player and a baseball player and the best hitter on the baseball team. And a nice kid. Shy, except with the other athletes, but friendly. Everybody liked him and they gave him a good hand when he went, grinning, up to get his diploma, and Mom and Pop sat among the relatives beaming, too.

"So," Pop said. "Our little boy. But not so little now, eh, Mother?"

Mom didn't answer right away. She was smiling and there were tears in her eyes and a little catch in her throat. Her boy. Only yesterday—it seemed—he was such a little fellow playing around the house. And now . . . that big, broad-shouldered boy. Why, he was almost a man. And now he was through with high school and would be going to Columbia. Her Lou to Columbia.

She turned to her husband and smiled again, and he patted her hand.

"A big boy, now, Papa," she said.

And so Lou left the school. One of many boys graduated that day. Better known than most of them, well liked by his teachers and by his coach, popular with his teammates. Yet no one could have dreamed then that he was to become the most famous graduate in the history of the school nor that for years he would be held up to the boys who came long after him as a model of all that a boy—or a man—should be. So that, more than twenty years later, a conversation such as this could take place—a conversation that, in its essence, must have been repeated many times over:

Bob Harron, in the athletic department at Columbia, was having his shoes shined by a little Negro boy on Broadway near the campus, and the boy asked him if he thought Columbia would beat Army on the approaching Saturday, and from that they fell to talking football generally, and Bob asked:

"Do you like to play football?"

"Yes, sir. I like it very much."

"And are you going to go to college?"

"Yes, sir."

29

"To Columbia?"

"No, sir. To Cornell."

"Why Cornell?"

"Because I know Brud Holland and he likes it so much there and has told me so much about it."

"Well," Bob said, "that's a good school, too. Are you going to high school now?"

"Yes, sir. I go to the High School of Commerce."

"Ah! Lou Gehrig's school."

"Yes, sir. Our teacher taught Lou Gehrig, and she tells us all about him and what a fine boy he was. And then what a fine man he was and how he used to come back to see her and the other teachers every chance he got. And how brave he was when that sickness was on him. . . . Did you know him, Mr. Harron?"

"Yes, I knew him very well," Bob said. "He was a fine man."

"Yes, sir. He must have been. They talk a lot about him down at school. And sometimes, when the boys get acting up a little, our teacher says:

" 'Lou Gehrig wouldn't have done like that. Lou liked to laugh and have fun and cut up, too. But he never did it in the classrooms. We never had the slightest trouble with him.'

"And when she says that, Mr. Harron, the boys quiet down. Because they all want to be like Lou Gehrig."

3. College Years

"I HOPE he has sufficient credits to enter the university," Bobby Watt had said the day he and Buck O'Neill discovered Lou as a football player.

He hadn't. However, within a few days after his graduation from Commerce he was admitted to the Department of Extension at Columbia, there to prepare himself for admission as a freshman in the fall. From the beginning he proved that he was an eager and serious student. His progress was rapid. There was no doubt that he would pass the extension course and the college board examinations.

As a student in the extension school, he was not eligible for participation in freshman athletics, but with the approach of the baseball season he asked Andy Coakley, the baseball coach, for permission to work out with the squad, volunteering to be of any help that he could, such as pitching in batting practice or shagging flies for the hitters. Coakley was not only willing but glad to grant the permission. He had heard about Lou as a high-school player. He liked the look of him and the size of him. He liked him even better when he saw him slamming the ball around South Field. Here, obviously, was varsity material in the making.

Lou was supremely happy that spring. He was at Columbia, he was progressing in his studies, and he was playing ball every day. He didn't like to withdraw from the field at the start of a game—Andy, after one good look at him, had told him to forget about the freshman and to work out with the varsity—but, after all, a fellow couldn't have everything right away. Things worth while were worth waiting for. His time would come. Meanwhile, it was great to be out there working with the varsity, hitting with the regulars in batting practice, working out at first base in the fielding practice after the regulars were through and just before the game started.

The course ended in June. The summer stretched ahead. It might seem long to him, but at the end of it he would be a regular freshman, eligible for the freshman football team. . . .

One day that summer Bobby Watt was in his office and Buck O'Neill called him on the telephone.

"Where's Gehrig?" he asked.

Bobby was surprised.

"Gehrig?" he said. "Why, I don't know. Home, I suppose. Working at some summer job. Why?"

O'Neill was silent for a moment. And then:

"You haven't heard anything?"

"Heard anything? What would I hear?"

"Well," Buck said, "I hear he is playing with the Hartford club of the Eastern League under the name of Lewis."

"What!"

"Take it easy," Buck said. "I don't know that it's true. But that's what I have heard. And, naturally, I am concerned because I want that young man to play football for me."

"So do I," Bobby said. "And I want him to play baseball for us, too. Who told you this?"

"A friend of mine."

"Have your friend call me," Bobby said. "I want to run this thing down as quickly as possible."

The friend called within an hour.

"Do you know this to be true?"

"I do."

34

"How do you know?"

"I saw him."

"When?"

"The other day."

"And you're sure you're not mistaken?"

"I talked to him."

"Thank you," Bobby said. "Thank you very much."

The next morning Bobby was on an early train for Hartford. He never had been to the Connecticut capital. Arriving there, he didn't know where to go to look for the boy until, of course, it was game time. He was strolling about and came to the park in front of the capital. There was Lou, sitting on a bench, head down, looking very disconsolate.

Bobby sat down next to him but said nothing. After a few moments Lou looked up. His eyes widened.

"Bobby!" he said.

"What are you doing here?" Bobby asked.

Lou was very uncomfortable.

"Playing ball."

"With the Hartford club?"

"Yes."

"Under the name of Lewis?"

"Yes."

"Why? Don't you know that you probably have

35

forfeited your amateur status and that you will not be able to play for Columbia?"

"No!" the boy cried. "No! They told me it would be all right!"

"Who told you that?"

"The—the—the baseball people. They said college players could play summer ball and it wouldn't affect their status as amateurs. They said all college players do it. And we need the money at home . . . and I believed them . . . and I thought it would be a good way to put in the summer. But I don't like it. I miss Mom and Pop. I . . . I guess I'm just homesick."

"How did all this come about, Lou? Who told you about this job in the first place?"

As they sat there on the bench, Lou told his side of the story.

He was leaving South Field after the last game of the season, he said, when a man approached him. A very pleasant chap. In his sixties, probably. White hair, close-cropped white mustache, ruddy-cheeked, smiling, immaculate.

"You're Lou Gehrig, aren't you?" he asked.

"Yes, sir."

"My name is Irwin," he said. "Arthur Irwin. I am a baseball scout. I've seen you working out here . . .

I understand you're not eligible for the team . . . and I like your work very much."

"Thank you," Lou said. "That's very nice to hear."

"Think you'd like to play professional ball?"

Lou laughed.

"Well, someday, perhaps," he said. "But I guess that day is a long way off. I want to go through college first."

"Of course," Irwin said. "But there is no harm in getting around and having somebody look at you. It might help a lot when you get ready to play professionally. . . . How would you like to work out with the Giants for a few days?"

"The Giants! The New York Giants?"

Irwin smiled.

"Exactly," he said. "I'd like to have John McGraw see you. I have an idea he might be interested in you."

The thought was exciting. John McGraw! The Giants!

"Why," he said, "I hardly know . . ."

"Suppose," Irwin said, "you meet me at the Polo Grounds at one o'clock tomorrow."

Lou nodded.

"All right," he said. "I'll be there, Mr. Irwin."

For four days he worked out on the Polo Grounds. John McGraw scarcely looked at him. The Giants were going badly, and McGraw was rasping at his players and had no time for a nondescript kid that Arthur Irwin had dragged in from some college field. McGraw didn't know what college field and didn't care.

"How do you like him, Mac?" Irwin asked at the end of the fourth day.

"Who?" McGraw demanded.

"That college fellow."

"Get him out of here," McGraw said.

"You mean you don't like him?"

"I don't even know what he looks like," McGraw said. "Here I am trying to get this team of mine straightened out, and you come around bothering me with a college player. I've got enough incompetents in Giant uniforms cluttering up the field without you bringing in another one."

"There is nothing around here for you right now," Irwin told the boy. "McGraw hasn't had a chance to look at you. He's too busy with his team."

"That's all right with me," Lou said. "I've had a chance to look at him . . . and listen to him. I wouldn't want to play ball for him."

Irwin shook his head.

"You've got him wrong," he said. "McGraw is one of the grandest men I've ever known—and I've known him for years. We used to play ball together, and in one way or another I have been associated with him ever since. You just happened to catch him at a bad time. Ask any of his ball players about him. He may yell at them when things are going bad, but there isn't one of them who wouldn't do anything in the world for him because they know he is the best friend they have."

"That may be true," Lou said. "But I don't like him."

Irwin laughed.

"Scared you a little, did he?"

"Maybe."

If McGraw had been indifferent to Lou, Irwin had been increasingly impressed with him.

"Want to go to Hartford?" he asked.

"What for?"

"To play ball, of course. With the Hartford team of the Eastern League."

"Wouldn't that bar me from playing college ball?"

Irwin shrugged.

"If it would," he said, "I guess there wouldn't be

39

any ball players left in the colleges. Most college players play summer ball to make a little money to pay for their tuition and books or to help out at home. . . . Could you use some money?"

"I should say I could."

"You're in," Irwin said. "Meet me at the Grand Central in the morning."

And so, with the assurance that everything was all right he had gone to Hartford and joined the ball club. But he didn't like it there, and he was homesick.

"There," he said. "That's the story."

"All right," Bobby said. "Now I'll tell you what you do. You tell them this afternoon that you're through. Then get your clothes together and come back to New York tonight with me."

"Am I through as a college player?" Lou asked anxiously.

"I don't know," Bobby said. "That isn't up to me. But you can bet I will go to bat for you and do everything I can to see that you're not ruled out."

On his return to New York, Watt took Lou's case up with the Columbia Athletic Council.

"At first glance," he said, "the boy's action may seem indefensible. He did go to Hartford and he did play with a professional team. However, I am convinced, having heard his story, that he believed this was quite the ordinary thing among college ball players. I also am convinced that if he had thought otherwise, he never would have taken the job.

"Ignorance of the law, they say, is no excuse. I don't believe that should be applied indiscriminately. I ask you to bear in mind that he never has taken part in athletics at Columbia and never has had occasion to familiarize himself with our rules."

He could see by the faces of the men around the board that he wasn't getting anywhere in particular.

"All right, then," he said. "Now, let me put it this way. It isn't sound technically or legally but here's what I think: I think that here is a fine, decent kid who has set his heart on playing baseball and football at Columbia. That for him to do so will enrich his life. And that for us to prevent him from doing so may embitter him. Good heavens, gentlemen, what did he do? He spent a couple of weeks in Hartford, he played a few games, he earned a few dollars that were badly needed at home. It isn't as though he were a regular professional ball player who was trying to put something over on us—or whom we were trying to use to put something over on our rivals. He

41

has broken the college rules, granted. But he is no better—and no worse—for having played those few games than he was when he walked off South Field in June. He's just a big, swell kid with his life before him and his way to make, and I don't think we would be serving a good end by making him pay for this mistake by forfeiting his entire college athletic career."

Now he could see he was on the right track. The members of the council began to discuss the case among themselves, to turn to him and ask him questions.

"Mind," he said, "it is my idea that we shouldn't deprive him of his entire career at Columbia. I do think we must take some action against him but that we must not be too severe. Here's what I propose: Let me write to all the colleges with whom we have baseball and football relations—and to any others with whom we might enter into negotiations during the next couple of years—tell them the truth, and ask them if they will permit us to play Gehrig against them provided we bar him from competition in his freshman year, which will start in September, and from baseball in his sophomore year. In other words, that his eligibility be suspended until the fall of 1922."

It seemed a reasonable solution. A compromise with the rules, of course. But a compromise prompted by the undeniably fine qualities of the boy involved. A vote of the council resulted in its unanimous adoption.

Watt communicated with Columbia's athletic rivals. The replies were prompt. Every one of them was to the effect that Columbia had handled a difficult situation sensibly and that Lou would be welcomed on the field of play in the fall of 1922—or before that, if Columbia wanted to lighten the sentence.

So, through his freshman year and the spring of his sophomore year Lou was permitted to work out in daily practice with the teams but had to remain on the sidelines when the games started. Naturally, there were times when it irked him to have to sit by when he felt it was his turn to hit or when there seemed to be a spot in which he should be carrying the ball. But he never complained.

He realized belatedly that he had made a sorry mistake when, having been approached by Arthur

43

Irwin—who (if he has been made to appear as the villain in the piece) was no villain at all but a hearty and pleasant old chap who merely did as any other scout would have done in the circumstances—he had not sought advice from Coakley or Watt. He realized with dismay how narrowly he had missed being banished from South Field so far as varsity competition was concerned, and he reflected that if he hadn't had a friend at court, he would not have had a chance at a university with a deserved reputation for strict adherence to the eligibility code.

So he never complained but practised faithfully—just as faithfully as he would have done had he been in the regular baseball and football line-ups. He had become a familiar figure on the campus among those who followed the athletic teams closely. They knew and liked this big, wavy-haired, smiling kid, who some day would reap honors on the baseball field and the gridiron for Columbia. And although he had first attracted attention there as a football player, it was as a baseball player that they knew him chiefly now. This was partly because they saw more of him in that role—secret practice screened most of his skill as a football player—and partly because he seemed to get more enjoyment from playing baseball than from football. But mostly it was a result of his daily practice on the diamond—he was the first out and the last in, and as the twilight gathered over the campus, he frequently could be found playing with groups of students who liked the game but were not sufficiently skilled in it to make the squad. He constantly was improving.

This was an accurate forecast of his competitive career at Columbia once it got under way. Contrary to a rather widely held opinion, which is that he was no great shakes as a football player, he was a very good one. Characteristically, he was willing to play anywhere, eager only to be of service to the team. Thus he played part of the time as a tackle and part as a halfback. As a lineman he hit hard on the offense and was stout and resourceful on defense. He preferred to play in the backfield, however—what kid, given his choice, wouldn't prefer to carry the ball or pass it or kick it to the grind of line play? Lou was a triple-threat man and in addition a fine blocker and a letter man on the 1922 team.

Probably the thing he did best, however, was to punt. Just as he was a long hitter in baseball, he could get tremendous distances with his punts, and long after his football days were behind him and he

45

was living in New Rochelle, he went, many an afternoon, to the high-school football field and spent an enjoyable hour kicking.

Bill McKenna, who has been football and baseball coach at New Rochelle High for many years and has developed numerous players who became famous in college competition, says of Lou:

"He was one of the best punters I ever saw. He never lost the knack of getting the ball away, he had a terrific leg drive and—which also figured in it—he never lost his enthusiasm. Our kids used to stand and gape at him as he would boot the ball down the field, and more than once I said to them:

" 'Don't get so lost in your admiration for him that you overlook how he is doing it. Take a good look at him. He's doing everything I have been trying to teach you fellows to do.'

"Which was so. He had perfect form and compared favorably with the best professionals I have seen— and I have seen all of them since the professional game became a major league sport."

But baseball—that was Lou's game. Harry Kane had discovered when he was in high school that Lou was weak against left-handed curve ball pitching and had worked hard with him and helped him to eradicate that weakness. On South Field, where he was looking at better pitching than he had seen in high school, right-handed curve ball pitchers bothered him at first. So Coakley had right-handed curve ball pitchers firing at him constantly in batting practice, and after a time he could straighten out any curve they threw at him.

When Lou began to play with the varsity in the spring of 1923, this had an amusing sequel. Coakley, just before a game one day, heard somebody tell the opposing coach to pitch curve balls to Lou because they were his weakness.

"When I heard that," Andy said, "I knew everything was going to be all right."

Sure enough, the opposing pitcher gave Lou a curve ball the first time he went to bat, and Lou flattened it for three bases. The coach must have thought that was an accident because the next time Lou went up he signed for another curve ball. Lou hit that one for a whistling single that drove two runs over the plate. By that time the coach must have concluded a mistake had been made somewhere, for he had his pitcher pitch fast balls to Lou, but, of course, that didn't do any good because Lou always could hit a fast ball. He wound up with four hits in four times at bat—but the hits he had made off the curve balls were the ones that really ruined the enemy.

Lou pitched, played first base and outfield for Columbia. This was no sign that Coakley didn't know where to play him or that he showed any weakness at first base. It simply was a sign that he was the most valuable man on the team and that Coakley shunted him around where, in a given game, he thought he would do the most good.

"Judged by college baseball standards," Andy said, "he was a fair outfielder and a good pitcher. In the outfield, he covered a lot of ground, got most of the drives hit his way, and had a strong arm and got the ball away fast. As a pitcher he didn't have much stuff, but he did have a better fast ball than most college pitchers and against certain teams he could just rear back and fire that fast ball all afternoon and win going away. There were days, too, when he seemed to have even more speed than usual. On such days no college team could beat him.

"However, in our more important games I used him at first base. That was where he really belonged because—again according to college standards—he was a good first-baseman. It is true that when he made the big jump from Columbia to the Yankees, they discovered there was a lot he had to learn about first-base play. These were the things he never could have learned in college baseball and the things that nobody could teach him because the only place to learn them is in the major leagues. But he was a very good first-baseman for us, and you could see, every step of the way, that he was going to get better as he went along and that some day, with proper training and experience, he might become a great one—which, of course, was what happened."

4. The Yankee Scout

IN the spring of 1923, at the training camp of the Yankees in New Orleans, a short, broad-shouldered, powerfully built man warmed up the pitchers before they took their turns in the box in batting practice or in one of the games between the regulars and the rookies. The chances are that Lou Gehrig never had heard of him.

This training camp bull-pen catcher was Paul Krichell, then, as now, chief of the Yankees' scouting force. Years before, he had caught for the St. Louis Browns and for numerous minor league clubs. Then, as now, he worked out with the Yankees every spring to keep himself fit for his job of stalking baseball talent in the raw through the minor leagues and the college towns. He had discovered some of the rookies in the camp this year. Those that he hadn't discovered were there because he had put the final stamp of approval on them.

And then the squad broke camp and started north, and Krichell moved north with them, and at last they were in New York and ready to open the season. And now Krichell was through with them for the season. His real work was to begin. Nowadays the Yankee office receives college schedules from all over the country, but in that time Paul, in a manner of speaking, worked at random, picking the games out of the daily schedules in the papers. And scanning a paper on a mid-April morning, he saw that Columbia was playing Rutgers at New Brunswick. If Fordham or New York University had been playing at home that day, Paul would have passed up the trip to New Brunswick, gone to see one of the other games, and waited for Columbia to play at South Field. But Fordham and N. Y. U. were idle that day.

"I might as well go to New Brunswick," Paul said to Edward Grant Barrow, then the Business Manager and now the President of the Yankees. "I might see somebody I like, although I haven't heard anything about either of those teams."

It happened that he caught the train that was bearing the Columbia team, and walking into the car reserved for the players he looked for Coakley and found him in a rear seat.

51

"Hello, Paul," Andy said. "It's flattering to see you with us. Whom are you after?"

Paul sat down, took out a cigar, and lighted it.

"I don't know yet," he said. "I'm just going for the ride, maybe. . . . Anybody on your ball club worth looking at?"

Coakley shrugged.

"We have a pitcher you might like," he said. "A big left-handed kid. He is a good hitter, too."

"A hitting pitcher, eh?" Paul asked. "And a left-hander."

"Yes."

"Is he going to pitch today?"

"He may," Andy said. "I don't know. I have another kid that may be ready. If he is, I'll start him."

"You wouldn't do an old friend a favor and start the left-hander, would you?" Paul asked.

"I'd like to," Andy said. "But I really want to save him for Pennsylvania on Friday."

"All right," Paul said. "I'll look at him then if he doesn't pitch today. You're playing Penn at home?"

"Yes."

Paul nodded.

"I'll be there, if necessary," he said.

When they reached the ball field at New Brunswick, Paul took his seat in the stands, and soon the game was under way. The other pitcher must have been ready, as Coakley had hoped, for there was a right-hander in the box for Columbia. Paul thought to watch him, but he soon forgot about him. There was a kid in right field who caught his eye. A broad-shouldered kid. A power-house hitter. A left-handed hitter who smashed the ball every time he stepped to the plate and twice hit home runs into the trees that bordered the field. That was his man. Never mind the left-handed pitcher Coakley had been talking about. Maybe he was good, too. But this kid in right field! That was the one he would go to South Field to see again on Friday. South Field! He'd go to the South Pole to have another look at a kid who could powder the ball like that! Why, Babe Ruth himself couldn't have hit a ball any better than the one he hit for his second home run.

The kid wasn't much of a fielder, seen through the eyes of a major league scout. He staggered around under a couple of fly balls, and Paul wasn't sure whether he would fall down or get hit on the head. He did manage to catch both of them. But his performance in the field was a triumph of tenacity over awkwardness.

53

Paul was on the station platform waiting for Coakley after the game.

"Who is that clown in right field?" he asked.

Andy laughed.

"I just wanted to see if you'd notice him," he said. "That's the kid I was telling you about. That's my left-handed pitcher."

"A pitcher!" Pal said. "A kid can hit like that—and you use him for a pitcher!"

"When it's his turn to pitch, I do," Andy said. "The rest of the time I play him in the outfield or on first base."

"So would I," Paul said. "I'd want that guy in my line-up in every game. What's his name?"

"Gehrig," Andy said. "Lou Gehrig."

"And he pitches against Penn on Friday?"

"Yes."

"I'll be there," Paul said.

That night Paul called Barrow on the telephone.

"Ed," he said, "I think I got something. I'm not sure yet. But I just want to see him do it again."

"Do what again?" Ed asked.

"Hit the ball like he hit at New Brunswick today. Ed—"

"Yes?"

54

"Ed, I think I've found another Babe Ruth!"

Barrow laughed.

"All right, Paul," he said. "Go to bed and get a good night's rest and you'll feel better in the morning."

"No, listen, Ed," Paul protested. "I'm not kidding. You know I don't talk like this as a rule. But I saw a kid today—"

"I know," Ed said. "Another Babe Ruth."

He laughed again and hung up.

On Friday Paul was at South Field. As his opponent on the mound that day, Lou drew Walter Huntzinger, the best college pitcher in the East that year, a tall, slim right-hander who subsequently joined the Giants. They waged an exciting duel. When Columbia went to bat in the ninth inning, the score was tied at 2-2—and Gehrig, wading into a fast ball, drove it out of the field and across 116th Street, where it bounded on the steps of the library.

As he jogged around the bases, the Columbia rooters swarmed out of the stands, picked him up, and carried him on their shoulders toward the dressing room in the basement of Furnald Hall, where Watt and O'Neill had talked to him nearly three years before. No wonder they were excited. The home run not only had won the game but it was the most amazing clout that ever had been seen on that field. It was a clout that they would talk about for years afterward.

Krichell struggled through the pack of delirious rooters, trying to reach Gehrig before he got down the steps to the dressing room. Pushing, panting, he finally made it.

"Lou!" he called. "Just a minute!"

Lou, beaming, laughing, turned to see who had called to him.

"Lou," Paul said, "I'm Paul Krichell. I scout for the Yankees."

Lou's eyes widened.

"Yes?" he said.

"Have you signed with any major league ball club?" Paul asked.

"Why, no," Lou said.

"Anybody else talk to you?"

"No. I never thought—"

"Well, I'm talking to you. I'm talking business to you right now. Would you like to play with the Yankees?"

Lou looked as though he couldn't believe what he had just heard.

"Are you serious?" he asked.

56

"Certainly, I'm serious," Paul said. "What do you think I'm doing? Amusing myself?"

"I'm sorry, Mr.—"

"Krichell."

"Mr. Krichell. I'm sorry. I didn't mean to offend you. But, you see, I never thought that anybody—I mean any big league ball club—would be interested in me. Especially the Yankees. Why—why—I don't know what to say."

"Well, take it easy, son," Paul said. "Would you like to talk to your coach first?"

"Yes, I would," Lou said. "Here's Andy now."

Andy was pushing his way through the crowd packed about the top of the stairs. When he saw Paul, he grinned.

"Well?" he said.

And turning to Lou:

"That was wonderful, Lou. The Babe himself couldn't hit one any better than that. . . . Have you signed with the Yankees yet?"

"Why, no, Coach," Lou said. "Mr. Krichell just asked me if I was interested, and I'd like to talk to you about it."

"Come in with us, Paul," Andy said.

"No," Paul said. "I'd rather you two talked it over

first. But I think I know how you'll advise the boy, and I'd like both of you to come to the office tomorrow morning and talk to Mr. Barrow. How does that suit you?"

"It sounds all right to me," Andy said. "What time?"

"How about ten o'clock?"

"Fine. We'll be there."

Paul shook hands with both of them and hurried across Broadway to the nearest telephone and called Barrow.

"I've got him, Ed!" he said.

"Who?" Barrow asked. "The second Babe Ruth?"

"Yes," Paul said. "And it's no joke. Are you familiar with South Field?"

"Yes."

"Well, today this kid pitched, went into the ninth inning tied at 2-2, and won his own game with a drive that not only went out of the field but across the street and landed on the steps of the library."

There was no raillery in Barrow's voice when he asked:

"And what about him—about him and our club?"

"Andy Coakley is going to bring him in to see you tomorrow morning."

"Fine," Barrow said. "Nice work, Paul."

Paul and Barrow were waiting at ten o'clock the next morning. But there was no sign of Coakley and Gehrig. Came ten-fifteen . . . ten-twenty . . . still no sign. Paul was getting nervous. Suppose Coakley, whom he knew to favor the boy's signing with the Yankees, hadn't been able to persuade him that that was the thing to do? Suppose the boy's parents didn't want him to play professional baseball? Suppose— Paul didn't know anything about the boy's family— suppose they had a lot of money and wouldn't be interested in the offer the Yankees were prepared to make him?

He paced Barrow's office nervously. Barrow looked up curiously from the papers on which he was working.

"I never saw you as steamed up as this about a kid before," he said.

"That's because I never saw a kid like this before," Paul said. "He's terrific, Ed. No fooling."

Just then the office boy came in.

"Mr. Coakley and another man to see you, Mr. Barrow," he said.

"Bring 'em in!" Paul roared.

The conference didn't last long. Terms were agreed

upon and Lou signed a Yankee contract. It was arranged that no public announcement be made of the signing at that time because Lou wished to finish out the college season.

"You'll report to us in June, then," Barrow said.

"Yes, sir," Lou said. "The day after our last game I will be at the Stadium."

"Good," Barrow said. "And good luck to you, young man."

It was a great day for Lou. It marked not only his signing as a Yankee but also the beginning of a friendship with Barrow that was to last all the days of his life.

5. Joining the Yankees

PAUSE for a moment and look at him as he enters the clubhouse in the Stadium to put on a Yankee uniform for the first time. He is twenty years old, six feet one inch tall, and weighs about 190 pounds. His hair is close cut and his face is lean. He is awed by his surroundings, for this is no ordinary ball club he is joining. These men, scattered about the clubhouse, getting out of their street clothes and into their uniforms, are the Yankees, twice pennant winners and on their way to a third pennant and the championship of the world. They have been in first place since the last week in April, and they are smashing along, steam-rolling the enemy.

The big guy with the muffin face, the huge chest, the skinny legs, and the booming voice is Babe Ruth. And that tall, lean, dour-looking fellow dressing next to him is Bob Meusel. The slim, smiling chap is Herb

Pennock. That light-haired, boyish one across the room is Waite Hoyt. Here's Wally Schang and there's Aaron Ward. That's Joe Dugan . . . and that's Joe Bush. That tall, quiet, serious-looking fellow is Wally Pipp, the first-baseman. The little fellow, that one with the dark hair and the Hoosier accent, is Everett Scott. Scott is the iron man of baseball. On May 2, in Washington, he had played his thousandth consecutive game, and Secretary of the Navy Denby, with President Byron Bancroft Johnson of the American League and the players of the New York and Washington teams looking on, had presented a gold medal to him in recognition of his remarkable achievement.

Gehrig stands there, looking about him, a little uncertain, a little lost. Doc Woods, the trainer, sees him and comes over to him.

"You're Gehrig, aren't you?" he asks.

"Yes, sir," Lou says.

Doc shakes hands with him and says he is glad to see him and then:

"This will be your locker over here. I put your stuff in the locker. Anything you want, just let me know. . . . Oh, meet the fellows. . . . Babe, this is Lou Gehrig from Columbia."

The Babe, who is lacing his shoes, looks up. The chances are he hasn't caught the name and wouldn't recognize it if he had. The Babe meets so many people and hears so many names that they do not mean anything to him. But he grins, sticks his hand out, and booms:

"How are you, kid!"

Kid. That's the Babe's name for every male person he meets, regardless of age. It will take him a little time to learn Gehrig's name. But the boy doesn't know that, and it wouldn't make any difference to him if he did. This is his hero. This is Babe Ruth and the Babe has greeted him cordially, and he feels more at home now and follows Doc around and shakes hands with the other players.

"Have you seen Hug yet?" Doc asks.

"No."

Doc leads the way across the big room to the manager's office. The door is closed and he knocks on it.

"Come in!"

They go in and Miller Huggins gets up from his chair in front of his roll-top desk. He is a little man. Spindly-legged, flat-footed, thin-faced, thin-lipped. He is in uniform and has been reading his mail. His

63

spectacles and a short-stemmed pipe lie on the desk beside a pile of letters.

"This is Lou Gehrig, Hug," Doc says.

Hug smiles and his eyes roam over the stalwart figure before him.

"You're a big fellow, aren't you?" he asks, as he shakes hands.

"Yes, sir."

"Good. I like them big."

He does, too. A little fellow himself and a great ball player in his day, he knows that it is not impossible for a little fellow to be successful in the major leagues. Johnny Evers was little, too, and Rabbit Maranville and others. But he would rather have them big.

"Sit down," he says.

Lou sits down and Hug asks him questions about himself. The boy doesn't know it but Huggins is prejudiced against college ball players. He came off the sandlots himself and he likes sandlot players. Oh, sure, some college players are all right. Look at Eddie Collins. Look at Frank Frisch. Look at Joe Dugan, his own third-baseman. And Matty was a college pitcher. And so was Jack Coombs. They could be good, of course. Could be great. But his

64

preference still ran to sand-lotters hardened in the minor leagues.

He likes the looks of this big kid, though. Likes the way he answers questions, likes his earnestness. Also, he likes the reports he has had on him from Krichell. Krichell is one of the top scouts of baseball, and when he goes out on a limb for a boy, as he has on Gehrig, the boy must have something.

The interview is brief. Lou goes out into the dressing room and puts on his uniform and knows the greatest thrill of his life. He is a Yankee. He is a teammate of Babe Ruth, Bob Meusel, Herb Pennock, Wally Pipp, Waite Hoyt, and all the others in that glamorous crew. He has a foothold in the major leagues. He must work hard to hold it and he knows it, but he has been working hard since he was a little boy and now the goal at which he is aiming is a brighter goal than any he has known before.

Somewhere in the back of his mind, perhaps, is the thought that this will mean comfort and security for his mother and father. But right now it must be that he is thinking:

"I am a Yankee! Look at me, Mom! Look at me, Pop! I'm a Yankee!"

The Little Dutch Boy had grown up.

By the time Lou had finished dressing, the other players had gone out on the field. Huggins came out of his office and, seeing him still in the clubhouse, asked:

"Do you know the way to the field?"

"No, sir," Lou said.

"Well, come on with me if you're ready."

Hug started for the door and Lou, with a last peek at himself in the mirror, hurried after him. Out the door and across the corridor and down the long, steep stairs. And then the short walk in the gloom under the big stand and, just ahead, the steps leading up to the dugout. Up the steps at the end of the dugout and then out on the field. The field at the Yankee Stadium . . . and the towering stands . . . and, out there at the batting cage, the Yankees. And he was a Yankee now, walking out to join his teammates and little Miller Huggins walking ahead of him.

He followed Huggins up to the cage, and Hug stood there watching the players hammer the ball about and then he said:

"Wait a minute, Joe."

It was Joe Dugan's turn to hit. Joe looked around. "Yes?"

"Let this young fellow hit a couple," Hug said.

Dugan stepped back from the plate.

"Get a bat," Hug said to Lou.

There were several bats lying on the ground back of the cage. Lou picked up the one nearest him and hustled up to the plate. The bat was long and heavy, even in his strong hands. He glanced at it and saw the name of Babe Ruth burned into it. He wanted to put it down and pick up another, fearful that he might split it if he wasn't holding it just right as he hit the ball. Everybody knew how the Babe prized his bats. How he notched a bat every time he hit a home run with it. But he didn't want to put it down in front of the players. They might see he was nervous, and he didn't want them to see that. He wanted them to think that he was perfectly at ease, going up there for his first swing at a ball in the Stadium.

The batting practice pitcher, skilled at throwing the ball where the players could hit it, threw a straight fast ball across the plate. Lou let it go. He was nervous now. More nervous, even, than he had thought he might be. All the Yankees standing there looking at him. Suddenly he was transfixed. The pitcher poured three more fast balls past him.

"Hit the ball," somebody said.

Lou dug himself in deeper at the plate. Now the pitcher pitched again and Lou swung and drove the ball on a line into right center. He had hit the ball squarely. In a ball game that would have been a base hit. His nervousness dropped from him. He had hit one. He was all right now. The feel of the bat in his hands as it met the ball had settled everything for him. No longer did he care whose bat it was he was swinging or who was looking at him. Another pitch . . . and another smash . . . another . . . another.

And now, as the ball players say, he really unloaded one. The ball soared into the bleachers in right center. It was a tremendous wallop.

There was a yell from the stand, just back of the Yankee dugout.

"Atta boy, Lou!"

The players looked around. Three young fellows— from Columbia, probably—were sitting in a box.

"Hit another one, Lou!" one of them yelled. "Show the Babe how to hit one."

"Looks as though he brought his own cheering section with him," Meusel said to Hoyt.

Lou hammered a ball that curled into the right field stand just inside the foul line.

68

"Hey," Dugan said. "What are you going to do? Stay up there all afternoon?"

"That's enough, Gehrig," Huggins said.

Lou stepped away from the plate, grinning.

"Sorry, Joe," he said.

Joe. A few minutes before he would have called the third-baseman Mr. Dugan. But he had hit two balls into the stands and he felt at home now. He was a Yankee, just like Dugan.

Huggins walked back to the dugout. He didn't say anything to Lou. But he knew the boy had it. That he was all Krichell had said.

The players knew it, too. Lou Gehrig had been nothing to them before that. Not even a name. Big league ball players do not pay much attention to college players. But when they saw him they knew he was a hitter.

"What's his name?" Whitey Witt asked Herb Pennock.

"Gehrig, I believe," Herb said.

"Where does he come from?"

"Columbia."

"Columbia, South Carolina?"

"No," Pennock said. "Columbia University."

69

"Oh. Well, he can hit, can't he?"

"I should say he can," Pennock said.

The players were taking their regular turns at the plate again. Lou picked up his glove and went to the outfield to shag flies.

"We all knew," Waite Hoyt said, a long time afterward, "that he was a big league ball player in the making. Nobody could miss on him. We didn't know what else he could do or in what position he would wind up. But it was a cinch that a young fellow who could hit like that couldn't be kept out of the major leagues."

When the Yankees' batting practice was over and Lou came in from the outfield to the dugout, Huggins beckoned to him.

"Yes, sir?"

"Big league ball players aren't made overnight," Hug said. "But you've got a lot to start with."

"Yes, sir."

"Go in and change your sweat shirt," Hug said, "and when the game starts, sit here with me. I want to tell you something about these fellows you will be playing against."

Lou was to know many thrills in the years that were beginning to unfold before him, but few were to match the thrill of that first afternoon in the Yankee dugout as he sat next to Hug and Hug said:

"Now, this fellow hits to right field. We pitch outside to him but once in a while he pulls one to right."

Or:

"This pitcher is tough to hit until you get a man on first base. Then he can't keep his mind off the runner and he isn't so tough. . . ."

6. Batting Slump in Hartford

LOU'S stay with the Yankees was brief. Huggins watched him closely, saw that he was a real slugger, and looked ahead to a day when he would be the Yankees' regular first-baseman. He put him into a game for the first time on June 16, when the Yankees were playing the St. Louis Browns, as a replacement for Pipp in the ninth inning because with the game safely won he wanted to see the young man in action briefly. Lou had one put out but did not get to the plate, of course, since the Yankees did not go to bat in the ninth.

Thereafter he was used as a relief first-baseman or pinch-hitter in twelve games. He hit major league pitching almost as well as he had hit that which he had found in the colleges, making eleven hits for a total of twenty bases and for an average of .423. He had acquitted himself even better than he had hoped or Huggins had expected. But the Yankees of 1923 had no room for a kid just breaking in. There was serious business at hand, business which only seasoned veterans were capable of handling.

That—1923—was the year in which the Yankees waged their fiercest fight against the Giants for the favor of New York fans. This had been held by the Giants since the contest had begun, in 1903, when the American League first invaded New York with a club owned by Frank Farrell, a gambler, and William S. Devery, former—and last—Chief of Police. The Giants, long entrenched in New York, were the ball club. Under the dynamic leadership of John J. McGraw, who had come to New York in 1902, the Giants won pennants in 1904, 1905, 1911, 1912, and 1913 and attracted great crowds, while the American League entry staggered along under a succession of managers. In 1915, however, the club was sold to Colonel Jacob Ruppert, brewer and sportsman, and Captain Tillinghast L'Hommedieu Huston, an engineer who, having fought in Cuba during the Spanish-American war, had remained there after the war and founded his fortune with the building of public works. They were friends of McGraw's and originally had wanted to buy the Giants, owned by the estate of John T. Brush, but the Giants were not for sale, and McGraw persuaded them to buy the American League club, which Farrell and Devery were eager to sell.

Ruppert and Huston bought the club, changed its name from Highlanders to Yankees, engaged Bill Donovan as manager, abandoned the old and outmoded grounds at 168th Street and Broadway, and moved into the Polo Grounds as tenants of the Giants. There could be, however, no quick turnover in the sentiment of the public. The Yankees still were merely the other team in New York—the team the fans went to see when the Giants were on the road. McGraw still was the dominant figure in baseball. His team, after a bad season in 1915 and a bad start in 1916, smashed back heavily, compiled two winning streaks as yet unsurpassed—seventeen games on the road in the spring and twenty-six at home as the season waned—and finished fourth in an exciting pennant race that was won by Brooklyn. In 1917 the Giants won the pennant, and they were favored to win again in 1918 and probably would have done so if they hadn't been crippled by the loss of players to the army.

Ruppert and Huston found they had a bitter

struggle on their hands but they were enthusiastic, resourceful, courageous, and—which was very important—they had plenty of money to spend and a great willingness to spend it. Thousands of the dollars they spent were wasted on players who were no good to them at all, but they refused to become discouraged. In 1917, Huston went off to war as Colonel of the Eighteenth Engineers, and very soon was in France. Ruppert, carrying on alone, released Donovan as manager and engaged Huggins, who had managed the St. Louis Cardinals in the National League. When word of this reached Huston in France, he was furious. He had not been unaware of an impending change of managers but his choice for the post was Wilbert Robinson, who had won the pennant with the Dodgers in 1916. He cabled his protests to Ruppert and Ruppert replied tartly. This was the beginning of a feud between them which was to result in Huston's eventual withdrawal from the club when, after years of wrangling, he accepted Ruppert's offer to buy his half of the stock.

Meanwhile, the war over and Huston back at his desk in New York, the partners continued spending huge sums to build up a winning club. The most fertile field for their operations was the Boston club, owned by Harry Frazee, theatrical producer. This club won the pennant and the world championship in 1918. By the spring of 1920 most of his better players, including Babe Ruth, were in Yankee uniforms. To climax the purchase of the players, Ruppert and Huston engaged Ed Barrow, who had managed the Red Sox, as business manager of the Yankees, and Barrow promptly began the creation of the most powerful organization in baseball.

Now the fight for patronage was reaching its peak. In 1921 the Giants and Yankees each won, and in the world series the Giants, after a slow start, came on to smash their rivals. In 1922 the teams again were the pennant-winners and in the world series the Giants again were triumphant, this time in four straight games, excluding a tie brought about by an impetuous umpire calling a game on account of darkness, although darkness had not yet descended.

Something else had happened, early in 1922, to make the Yankees' defeat in the world series especially galling to Ruppert and Huston. The triumvirate controlling the Giants (Charles A. Stoneham, who had purchased control of the club from the Brush estate in 1919, McGraw, and Francis X. McQuade, pal of Stoneham and McGraw and treasurer of the club) decided they wanted the Polo Grounds for the Giants alone. The growth of the Yankees with the coming of Ruth, Huggins, and Barrow had roused a fierce resentment in the camp of the Giants. The Yankees, virtually ejected from the Polo Grounds, were constructing the Stadium on the opposite bank of the Harlem during the summer of 1922. They were to open it in the spring and hoped to hoist the world-championship flag over it on opening day, but this hope was shattered by the Giants' one-sided victory in the series.

Now it was 1923, and both Yankees and Giants were driving hard toward a third world series in New York. It was into this scene that Gehrig was projected the day he walked into the Yankee clubhouse, but there was no part for him in it. Later, in equally stirring scenes, he was to play a major part, but now he was young and inexperienced and had to be trained for the part he was to play. And so he was sent to—of all places—the Hartford club of the Eastern League on option. This meant that he still belonged to the Yankees, of course, and could be recalled at any time.

He finished the season in Hartford, playing first base in fifty-nine games, hitting .304, and contributing to the winning of the pennant. His roommate with the Hartford club that year was Charles Swaney, a left-handed pitcher. Lou thought he was a good pitcher and someday would be in the major leagues, but he never made it. Years later, as a member of the bearded House of David team, he pitched against the Yankees in an exhibition game at their training camp in St. Petersburg, Florida, and struck Lou out twice. Lou still thought he was a good pitcher.

Only once during that summer in Hartford did Lou falter. When he did, he was straightened out in a manner that reflects the working of the Yankee organization.

He had been there but a short time when he fell into a batting slump. For two or three days he struggled hard to come out of it, and when he failed he began to worry. When he did that, his fielding fell off and he was in a very bad way indeed. He began to believe that Hartford was a hard luck town for him. All the memories of his ill-advised and ill-starred adventure in Hartford in 1921 surged up within him. The old homesickness that had assailed him two years before engulfed him again.

Pat O'Connor, manager of the Hartford club, having watched him anxiously for a few days, saw him go from bad to worse, noted the droop of his powerful shoulders and the harried look on his face, and wired to Ed Barrow:

"Gehrig no use to this ball club. Please recall him."

Barrow read the wire and pressed a button on his desk. One of the office force came in.

"Where's Paul Krichell?" Barrow asked.

"Spartanburg, S. C."

"Wait a minute," Barrow said.

He wrote out a telegram and handed it to the young man.

"Get this right off," he said.

Krichell, in Spartanburg to scout some players in the South Atlantic League, received the wire an hour later. It read:

"Proceed at once to Hartford. Gehrig in a bad slump. Talk to him."

"The words Ed Barrow uses mostly," Paul has said, "are 'at once' and 'immediately.' And he isn't fooling."

Krichell was on the next train leaving Spartanburg

79

for New York. He crossed the town from the Pennsylvania Station to the Grand Central and was on the first train for Hartford. He was in time for the ball game and went directly to the park. Neither O'Connor nor Gehrig knew he was there. He sat up in the stand and watched Gehrig closely. Lou had another bad afternoon. He failed to get a hit in four times at bat and while he made no errors at first base his play was lackadaisical.

"He had his chin on his chest all afternoon," Paul said.

After the game he waited for Lou, who naturally was surprised to see him.

"What are you doing here?" he demanded.

"I came up to see you, you big stiff," Paul said. "What's the matter with you, anyway?"

Lou shook his head.

"I don't know," he said. "I just can't seem to get going."

"Well," Paul said, "forget about it for the moment and let's go downtown and see what we can do to a couple of steaks."

They went down to the Bond Hotel and had a good dinner, during which they talked about everything but Lou's slump. And then, when Paul had his

coffee before him and had lighted a cigar, he said:
"Now, then. What's this all about?"

Lou, more than glad to talk to somebody he knew,
poured out his story. Two hitless days . . . a sleepless
night . . . no hits for two more days . . . less sleep
. . . homesickness . . . worry over his job . . . humilia-
tion because, having been hailed by the Hartford
newspapers on his arrival as the Great Gehrig and
Columbia Lou, the Fence Buster, he had failed so
miserably.

Paul listened to him patiently, never interrupting
him, letting him spill his somber thoughts as they
crowded his mind. It was an old story to Paul. He
had heard it from the lips of countless young ball
players. Maybe it took him back to his own youth
and the days when he was trying to make a place for
himself in the big leagues and knew days of doubt
and uncertainty and couldn't sleep at night and
wished to God he was home.

And when at last Lou had finished, Paul said to
him:

"I know just how you feel. But you've got to get
over it. And right away. So you didn't make any hits
for two days. So what? Who do you think you are,
anyhow? The greatest hitters I've ever known—and

I've watched them come and go—have had two, three, four, five, and even six hitless days in a row. Don't you know that?"

"I guess so, but—"

"But you're going to get some hits every day, eh? Well, you're not. Look at the batting averages. We say a fellow who hits .300 is a good hitter, don't we? And a fellow who hits .350 is a terrific hitter, while .400 hitters come along very rarely. Well, what does that mean?—that the greatest hitters the game ever knew hit around .400, which means that they made four hits in every ten times at bat. And don't forget that old law of averages. Sure, you know. You've heard all about it. You know it's the one law nobody can beat. And what happens? You've got your dauber down right now because you're not able to beat it. You've had days, in the beginning up here, when you made three or even four hits, haven't you?"

"Yes."

"Well, did it ever occur to you that the law of averages must work out so that you will have days when you won't get any hits at all."

"Yes. I know that, Paul. But not as many days as I've had lately."

"That's what I'm getting at," Paul said. "You

shouldn't have had as many. But after you had two, you began to worry—and when you got well into your worrying, you didn't have a chance to get out of your slump. Ever hear of Ty Cobb?"

Lou smiled.

"It seems to me I have," he said. "He plays with Detroit, doesn't he? An outfielder, or something?"

"Yes," Paul said, "and a fair country hitter. Well, do you know what Ty told me once when I asked him what he did when he got into a slump—or does it surprise you, Mr. Gehrig, that Cobb gets into slumps once in a while, too?"

The furrows had left Lou's forehead, and he was able to laugh again.

"What did he say?" he asked.

"He said that he didn't worry because he was in a slump. He knew he was a good hitter, that slumps were inevitable, and that he would come out of it in a few days. He figured the reason he was in a slump was that his stroke was off—that instead of hitting straight at the ball he was hitting down or up. So, without even trying to get a base hit, he concentrated on trying to hit the ball back to the pitcher because he knew in that way he would readjust his stroke. And in a couple of days he was hitting again."

"That sounds reasonable," Lou said.

"Reasonable!" Paul said. "Why, its some of the soundest baseball you ever listened to, you lug. . . . Feel better now?"

"I sure do. And I'm very grateful to you, Paul."

"Forget that part of it," Paul said. "That's what I'm hired to do. Not only to find young ball players but to straighten them out when they get into trouble."

He looked at his watch and then consulted a time-table.

"I've spent all the time I'm going to with you," he said. "I'm going to dash back to New York and spend a night at home for a change before I hit the road again in the morning."

They walked down to the station, and Lou waited with Paul for the train. As he was about to board it, Paul shook hands with Lou and said:

"Get a good night's sleep—and tomorrow start hitting the ball back to the pitcher. And whenever you fall into a slump again, remember what Hank Gowdy once said."

"What was that?"

"He said: 'The most important thing a young ball player can learn is that he can't be good every day.'"

"All aboard!" the conductor cried.

"So long," Paul said. "I'll be watching you through the newspapers. Let me see you start hitting in a couple of days."

"I will," Lou said.

He did

7. Spring Training in New Orleans

RECALLED from Hartford at the close of the 1923 season and ordered to report at the training camp, then in New Orleans, in the spring of 1924, Lou was a step nearer a regular job with the Yankees, and his eyes, and his mind, were on the future. Things were picking up at home, too, but slowly. The money he had made playing ball came in handy, but there were so many old debts and new bills to be paid that when the time came for him to leave for New Orleans the last week in February of 1924 he had only twelve dollars in his pocket.

A ball player during the spring training season has all his expenses, even including his laundry, paid by the club. But he must have money for tips and other incidentals, and Lou had twelve dollars to cover a six weeks' span. Having little or no money to spend on himself was no hardship to him. He had been used to that state of affairs all his life. But he was worried this time. No matter how careful a fellow was, he was going to have a hard time getting by on so little on a six weeks' stay with a major league club.

There was a young catcher on the club that year. A young fellow named Benny Bengough, whose home was in Buffalo and who had been purchased by the Yankees from the Buffalo club in midseason of 1923. He and Lou roomed together and thus began a friendship that ended only with Gehrig's death.

Benny, a chunky little fellow, lively, laughing-eyed, and already rapidly becoming bald although he was only twenty-six years old, was unusually quiet one morning.

"What's the matter with you?" Lou asked.

"Nothing," Benny said.

"Come on, open up."

"Well," Benny said, "I'm broke. Or practically so. I've got about fifteen dollars but, Gee, it's a long way to go to that first pay day."

Lou had said nothing to Benny about his own financial status, fearing that his roommate might look down a fellow with so little money. He was greatly relieved to discover that Benny wasn't much better off than he was.

87

"Why," he said, grinning, "you're not practically broke. You're practically wealthy. Do you know how much I have?"

"No."

He took his money out and counted it.

"Nine dollars and thirty-five cents," he said. "I had twelve dollars when I left home."

"And that's all you have?"

"Yes."

Benny looked at him.

"What are we going to do?"

Lou hesitated for a moment. And then:

"You know, I had a crazy idea last night. Or maybe it wasn't so crazy at that . . . I . . ."

"What?"

"Well," Lou said, "I was taking a walk after dinner, and about a mile out on Canal Street I saw a pretty good looking restaurant. I looked in the big windows and saw the people eating and drinking and the waiters hurrying around and it gave me an idea. I thought I might go out there and see if I couldn't get a job waiting for a couple of hours in the evening at the height of their dinner hour. I could eat right after practice and get out there and work until ten o'clock. I used to wait on table in a fraternity house at Columbia, and I thought maybe I could make a couple of dollars a night. . . . Would you want to try it with me?"

"Sure," Benny said, his face brightening.

"Of course," Lou said, "we might not get the job."

"And if we do," Benny said, "I might drop a plate of soup down somebody's neck because I never had any practice at waiting on table. But they can't shoot a guy for that, can they?"

"I don't think so," Lou said. "Anyway, we'll give it a try."

They had their dinner about five-thirty that evening and walked out Canal Street.

"This is the place," Lou said.

They stood outside for a few minutes, trying to get up nerve enough to enter. It never occurred to them that prospective waiters probably should have gone around to the back, or kitchen, door. They had thought only of walking in, asking for the manager, and bracing him for jobs.

"Well," Lou said. "We'll never get anywhere standing here. And we do need the dough. So come ahead."

89

"I'll follow you," Benny said.

They walked in and the headwaiter came smiling to meet them.

"Good evening," he said. "Two?"

"Is the . . . er . . . we'd like to see the manager," Lou said.

The headwaiter's eyebrows went up like twin elevators.

"The manager?" he said. "Why, sir? Is anything wrong?"

"No," Lou said, "but we—"

Benny tugged at his arm and began to move toward the door.

"Out!" he said. "Quick! Out!"

Lou was bewildered.

"Out?"

"Yes. Quick."

Now Benny was in full flight. Lou looked helplessly at the headwaiter.

"I don't understand, sir," the headwaiter said. "I thought you—"

"I don't understand, either," Lou said. "But good-by."

He hurried into the street and looked around for Benny.

"Hey, Lou!"

Benny's voice came from a doorway in the next building.

Lou quickly joined him.

"What's the matter with you?" he asked. "Are you going nuts? It's a wonder the fellow didn't think we were planning to stick the place up and yell for the cops."

"Didn't you see them?" Benny asked.

"See them? Who? The cops?"

"Cops! No!" Benny said. "Didn't you see who were at a table on the right as we went in?"

"No. Who?"

"Pennock, Meusel, Dugan, and Hoyt!"

Gehrig was shocked.

"No!" he said. "Did they see us?"

"I don't know," Benny said. "I don't think they saw me, but they may have seen you."

By now they were walking rapidly in the direction of the hotel.

"What will they think if they did?" Lou asked.

"Well," Benny said, "they'll hardly think a couple of bushers were going to eat and drink in a place like that."

He stood still and laughed.

91

"We certainly got off lucky," he said. "Suppose we had been there early and got the jobs and they'd come in and sat at your table or mine—or seen us standing around with those monkey suits on!"

Gehrig continued to improve in the spring of 1924. In the practice games between the regulars and the youngsters he was on first base for the youngsters. Before the games and frequently when they were over, he worked out at the bag. There was much he had to learn, but Huggins and the other players were both helpful and patient with him.

No one helped him more than Wally Pipp. Tall, light-haired, blue-eyed, and an extremely able first-baseman, Wally knew that he was nearing the end of his string as the regular first-baseman of the Yankees. A graduate of Georgetown University, he had entered professional baseball in Grand Rapids, Michigan, his home town, in 1910, and so there were fourteen years of play behind him when he went South with the Yankees that spring. He wasn't through, but he knew he didn't have much further to go, at least with the Yankees. Not with this wide-shouldered, eager, determined kid being readied to take his place. This kid who could hit with such terrific force and to whom all kinds of pitching looked alike.

Instead of resenting Gehrig's presence on the squad, Pipp went out of his way to help him.

"No," he would say, as Lou made an awkward play in practice. "Not that way. This way."

He would show him an easier, surer way to make the play, and Gehrig would watch him and try to copy his style and after a while he would get it, and then Pipp would have him make the play over and over again and one day he said:

"Well, young fellow, I will say this for you: You may not learn fast, but once you learn you don't forget."

Huggins would talk to him, sometimes on the field, sometimes in the clubhouse or the lobby of the hotel. Huggins, wise, thoughtful, and genuinely interested in all the young men who played for him, not only as ball players but as youngsters tussling with life, was especially interested in this young giant from the sidewalks of New York. Any prejudice he might have felt toward him because he was a college ball player long since had been dissipated. He knew that here was a ball player who not only would be a true major-leaguer in another year or so but also one who, if nothing happened to him along the way, might know greatness one day.

He talked to him about his mother and father, about his financial problems, gave him sound advice and endless encouragement. He already was exerting a tremendous influence on him, and in after years Lou could look back and realize that here was a man who had helped tremendously to fashion his life. A man whom he not only respected but for whom he had a great and abiding affection.

One day, as the Yankees prepared to break camp and start on the two weeks' exhibition trip that would take them to New York, Huggins called Gehrig to his room.

"Sit down, Lou," he said.

This was the first time Lou had been in the manager's room. He could guess what Huggins wanted to see him for. He wanted to tell him he was being sent to the minor leagues again.

"I am going to send you out again," Huggins said. "I'm sending you back to Hartford."

Well, there it was. He hadn't been very confident of remaining with the Yankees that season. He knew that he hadn't been able to replace Pipp. Replace Pipp? Why, he couldn't carry Pipp's glove! Still, he had hoped that somehow he might stay. That Huggins might keep him on the bench and use him now and then when Pipp was tired or when a game was palpably won or hopelessly lost. But this was it. Definitely. He was going out again.

His disappointment—and although he had tried to prepare himself for the news he was disappointed—must have been reflected in his face, for Huggins smiled at him.

"Don't feel badly about it," he said.

"I don't," Lou said. "I know I don't belong with this club and—"

"Don't say that," Huggins said. "You belong very much with this club. But this is why I am sending you out for another year: Wally Pipp still is a good first-baseman and will be in there every day this year, which means that if I kept you, you would not be able to play unless I wanted to stick you in for an inning or so once in a while. And that's no way for a young fellow to learn. I am sending you to Hartford where you will be playing every day and be up there at the plate taking your swing, and it will do you a lot of good. And I promise you this: when you come back in the fall, you will come back to stay. This is your last year in the minors. And remember that I will be thinking about you and watching you in the box scores, and I have no doubt that you will have a great year."

He got up and put out his hand.

"Thank you, Mr. Huggins," Lou said. "I won't disappoint you."

"I know you won't," Huggins said, walking to the door with him. "Incidentally, you are not going to the Hartford club just yet. I just wanted you to know what I had in mind. You are going through to New York with us and I will keep you around for a little while after the season opens."

He smiled and patted Lou on the shoulder.

"I want to give you a little more practice shooting at the right-field bleachers," he said.

Lou journeyed north with the Yankees and was with them when they opened the season in Boston. From there they went to Washington and then to the Stadium for the home opening. He stayed around for a while, saw service as a pinch-hitter, played a few innings at first base, went to bat twelve times in ten games, and made six hits for an average of .500. And then he was off to Hartford.

He didn't disappoint Huggins in Hartford. Playing 134 games at first base, he had a batting average of

.369. Half of the 186 hits were for extra bases, thirty-seven of them were home runs. He was ready for the big leagues.

8. 1925—Lou Becomes a Regular

THE 1925 season was a bad one for the Yankees. Beaten off by the Senators in 1924 after they had won three pennants in a row and climaxed the winning of the third pennant with a victory over the Giants in the 1923 world series, they managed to finish second, and Huggins had high hopes of driving them back to the top of the league with the coming of another season.

The first blow to his hopes came with the sudden and frightening illness of Babe Ruth when the team, bound northward from the training camp, reached Ashville, North Carolina. The Babe was stricken with a stomach ailment (the late W. O. McGeehan, one of the top sports writers of all time, described it as the world's greatest tummy-ache because it had so many repercussions) and was placed, moaning, on a train for New York. The news startled fans all over

98

the country. Some of the newspapers in New York wired to their correspondents accompanying the team to leave the team and accompany the Babe. When, attended by reporters and met by other reporters, camera men, and a muddle of fans, he arrived in the Pennsylvania Station, he was rushed to St. Vincent's Hospital.

The first stories emanating from the hospital—which, it developed, were rumors and not the reports of the physicians who examined him—were that he never would be able to play ball again. These soon were corrected, but it was made clear that the Babe was a pretty sick man and would have to rest for a few weeks at least. And so for a few weeks he was the pale and pallid invalid, taking his liquid nourishment—and his reports of the ball games—in a wheel chair. The reports weren't very encouraging. The team that had won three times in a row and then finished second in a driving race was wearing out. Huggins began to shuffle his players, to make changes in the line-up, to resort to every means at his command to rekindle the fire that had made the Yankees champions. But no matter what he did, the Yankees remained about as they were.

Then the Babe recovered and returned to the

line-up. Now, everybody said, the Yankees would step out. But they didn't. The Babe was no help whatever. He couldn't get going, either. And then the Yankees were in St. Louis and things still were going badly and the Babe was hitting .246 when there was a terrific row in the clubhouse between Huggins and the Babe. The upshot of it was that Huggins, who had charged the Babe with violating the training rules, suspended him and fined him $5,000. No ball player ever had been fined $5,000 before. But, then, there never had been a Babe Ruth before. Huggins, never an unreasonable man, explained that since the Babe was no ordinary ball player, no ordinary fine would have an effect on him. And, in those trying days, Huggins was determined not only to whip the Babe back into line but to make the other players understand clearly that not even the Babe could flaunt his authority and go unscathed.

Ruth left the ball club, stormed back to New York, and announced that he never would play under Huggins again.

"It's me or him," he told reporters who met him at the train. "If they want him to manage the club, they got to sell me or trade me or something."

100

"And what are you going to do next?" the reporters asked.

"I'm going to see Jake," he said.

Jake was Colonel Ruppert. The day that he had bought out Colonel Huston he had walked into the clubhouse and addressed the players briefly. Some of the players, taking advantage of Huston's known hostility to Huggins, openly had defied the manager, believing that if he disciplined them they had only to appeal to Huston to have their fines or suspensions revoked. Ruppert wanted to set them straight.

"Gentlemen," he said, "I have just become sole owner of this ball club. Miller Huggins is my manager."

And with that he walked from the room.

Now, for the first time since that fateful day, Huggins' authority had been challenged—and in dramatic fashion. And the Babe was on his way to see Jake, with a string of reporters at his heels.

The interview, which took place in the Colonel's office in his brewery at Ninety-second Street and Third Avenue, did not last long. When it was over the reporters were admitted and saw a chastened Ruth.

101

"Gentlemen," the Colonel said. "Mr. Ruth no longer wishes to be sold or traded. He has accepted his suspension and will pay his fine."

The reporters looked at the Babe.

"That's right," he said. "I spoke a little too quick. I will go on playing for Huggins as soon as he reinstates me, and I am sure we will not have any more trouble."

It wasn't long before the Babe was back in the line-up. He did the best he could. He hammered and hammered away and drove his batting average up to .290 by the end of the season, but there wasn't anything he or Huggins or anybody else could do to save the Yankees that year. They finished seventh. It was the worst showing the club ever had made since the Ruppert-Huston renaissance, and that winter, at the Baseball Writers' dinner, it achieved a virtual immortality when Rud Rennie of the *Herald-Tribune*, impersonating the Colonel and his soft German accent sang to the tune of "You Wonderful One":

> *You wonderful two, how I dote upon you,*
> *Ed Barrow, so handsome and tall.*
> *And wee Little Hug, just so small like a bug,*
> *There are thousands can't see him at all.*

102

And though I am blue, I give credit to you,
With my cash you have made me a dub.
I wanted a winner. As I am a sinner,
You gave me a seventh place club.

The domination of the American League by the Yankees had ended in 1924. A threat of its restoration had been smashed in 1925, the black year of the Ruppert regime.

The black year? Well, yes. And yet, on June 1, 1925, something happened that was to have a tremendous effect on the future of the Yankees and the record of which was to be written large in the history of baseball.

On that June day—too much like too many other days the Yankees had known and were to know that year, which is to say that the Yankees were losing, this time to the Senators—Lou Gehrig was sent up as a pinch-hitter for Pee Wee Wanninger, the short stop. He didn't make a base hit, and nobody thought anything about it and the baseball writers made but a hasty and passing note of it in their books. They would have been more than mildly excited, however, if they had known that they were checking off the

103

appearance of Gehrig in the first of a string of 2,130 consecutive games. For that, as a research begun several years later revealed, was the beginning of the greatest endurance record that baseball ever has known and, in all likelihood, ever will know.

The following day, Lou reported at the Stadium, got into his uniform, took batting and field practice, and then went to the clubhouse to change his shirt. As game time approached the regulars drifted out of the clubhouse toward the dugout, but Lou was in no hurry since he had nothing to do but sit on the bench and watch the game. He had just stretched himself out on a rubbing table when Huggins came out of his office.

"Tired?" he asked.

Lou, an embarrassed grin on his face, sat up.

"No," he said.

"Good," Huggins said. "You're playing first base today."

He walked out of the clubhouse, and Lou, startled and even scared a little, grabbed his mitt and followed him.

Pipp hadn't been going too well, and Huggins had thought that a few days rest would do him good. That, at least, was what he told Pipp. It may have been that he had reached the conclusion that the time had come for him to replace Wally with the strong-armed, belting kid from Columbia. Whatever Huggins had said—whatever he had thought—the time had come.

Gehrig went to bat five times that day, made three hits, scored one run, had eight put-outs, and one assist. Pipp never returned to first base.

Lou hit .295 that year. Among his hits were twenty-one home runs. Obviously, he was on his way. And yet, so many had been the changes in the Yankees that year and so poor their fortunes that he drew much less attention than some of his teammates from the chroniclers in the press box. Most of this went to the Babe's fall and rise. Also of interest were the replacement of Wally Schang back of the plate by Lou's pal, Benny Bengough; the withdrawal of Whitey Witt from center field to make room for Earle Combs, the handsome youngster up that year from Louisville; and the benching, at long last, of Everett Scott, who had played in 1,307 games without a break—a record that was to stand until Gehrig, still riding the pine in the dugout the day Scott was benched, broke it.

The almost casual reception by the newspapers of

his elevation to a regular post didn't disturb Lou in the least. He was happier than he ever had been before. He was a Yankee now in all truth. Out there at first base every day, playing in every game. Not having to sit on the bench through the long afternoons hoping that, somehow, he might break into the game if only as a pinch-hitter or to play a single inning.

He wasn't getting enough ball playing to suit him, however, even on days when the Yankees played double-headers. For no one ever liked to play ball any more than he did or hated more to quit on any given day as darkness closed about him. Darkness seldom closed about him at the Stadium or when the team was on the road, and he found a way to put in an hour or two of extra play during the home stands. He played in the streets with the neighbors' kids.

For these twilight pavement performances, he wore a sweat shirt, an old pair of pants, and baseball shoes from which he had pried the spikes. And every evening, after his dinner, he would be out there hitting to the kids and having a lot of fun. And then one night there was the shrill cry of:

"Cheese it! The cops!"

Some of the neighbors, annoyed by the crack of

Lou's bat and the shouts of the boys, had complained, and now three cops were closing in on the players. Some of the kids dusted out of sight. The others, trapped, stood there petrified with fright.

"And you, you big gawk," one of the cops said to Lou. "You're worse than the others because you're old enough to know better."

The round-up was completed, and the captives were marched off to the near-by stationhouse. The desk lieutenant looked up at the array.

"These are the ones that were playing ball in the street," one of the arresting officers said.

"Oh, yes," the lieutenant said.

He opened his blotter, which is what the police call the book in which arrests are entered, and glared at Gehrig, towering among his fellow prisoners.

"The leader of the gang, I suppose?" he said.

"Yes, sir," Lou said.

"Your name?" pen poised for writing.

"Henry Louis Gehrig."

"Henry Louis— What?"

The pen was uplifted.

"Gehrig."

"Gehrig? Lou Gehrig?"

"Yes, sir."

107

"The ball player?"

"Yes, sir."

"The Yankees' first-baseman?"

"Yes, sir."

The lieutenant dropped his pen and stuck his hand over the desk.

"I'd like to shake hands with you, young fellow," he said. "I saw you play yesterday. You're a great ball player, my boy."

The arresting officers stared at him. The kids were grinning from ear to ear. The lieutenant turned on the policemen.

"A fine lot you are," he said. "Dragging Lou Gehrig in like this. Have you no brains entirely?"

"We didn't know who he was, Lieutenant," one of them said. "Why didn't you tell us, Lou?"

Lou laughed.

"There didn't seem to be any reason to tell you," he said. "You caught me red-handed, along with my pals, and you had to arrest me, didn't you?"

"Well, there had been complaints and—"

"Forget it!" the lieutenant said. "Tell me, Lou, how about the Babe? Is he going to come back all right? What about this young fellow Combs? How does it feel to hit against Walter Johnson?"

108

The cops had questions of their own. Lou was kept busy answering them for an hour. Finally he said:

"Are you going to lock us up?"

"Ain't you the one!" the lieutenant said. "Lock you up? Get on with you!"

"Then may I take my pals home? I think it's time they were in bed."

"Certainly," the lieutenant said.

He came around from behind the desk to shake hands with Lou again. He and the cops escorted the erstwhile prisoners to the door.

"Come and see us again soon," the lieutenant said. "And, if you don't mind, Lou, please don't play ball in the streets any more. There have been complaints, and if you don't stop, you will get us in bad here."

"I promise," Lou said. "And I can promise for the boys, too. It was all my fault, because they were playing only because I asked them to. Hereafter I'll confine my playing to the Stadium, and the boys will stick to the parks and playgrounds . . . Good-by . . . and thanks a million."

"You're welcome," the lieutenant said. "And good luck to you, Lou."

9. Ruth, Gehrig, and Meusel

AT St. Petersburg in the spring of 1926, Miller Huggins set about rebuilding his team. With Ruth once more in good condition after a winter of rest and golfing, with Bob Meusel at the top of his form and Earle Combs hardened by a season in the majors, the outfield was set. Benny Bengough was complaining of a lame arm, but Huggins had a young catcher named Pat Collins and the veteran Hank Severeid to do the receiving. He had a good pitching staff—Herb Pennock, Waite Hoyt, Urban Shocker, Sam Jones, Bob Shawkey, Dutch Ruether, and Myles Thomas. His chief concern was with the infield. There he had to gamble.

For first base he had Gehrig and for third base the veteran Joe Dugan. Gehrig had made a great beginning the year before, and Huggins wasn't worried about him in spite of his scant experience as a big league regular. And he didn't even have to think about Dugan, for Joe was the best third-baseman in either league. But to win a pennant or even to stay up in the race as the summer rolls on, a team must be strong at short stop and second base. And here Huggins had a couple of kids. The short stop, Mark Koenig, had been brought up from St. Paul near the end of the 1925 season. The second-baseman, Tony Lazzeri, was fresh from the Salt Lake club of the Pacific Coast League and never had seen a major league game.

"If those kids fail me," Huggins said, "we'll wind up in sixth place. If they come through, we'll win the pennant."

The critics scoffed at him. The Yankees win the pennant with two bushers around the middle bag— and, for that matter, with a fellow who was little more than a busher at first base? Oh, sure, Gehrig was all right last year. But there was no pressure on him then. This time it was going to be different, with Huggins in the dugout mumbling about a pennant.

Only one of the critics believed him. Fred Lieb echoed the Little Miller's sentiments. If Koenig and Lazzeri stood up, the Yankees would win the pennant, he wrote. The others thought he suddenly had gone balmy—and predicted the Yankees would finish sixth.

Once the season got under way, it looked as if Huggins might be right. He got good pitching, Koenig made a fair start at short stop, Lazzeri was a revelation at second base, playing with the poise of an old-timer, and the infield was securely anchored with Dugan at third base and Gehrig at first. The pitching was good and the catching, as the dramatic critics would say, was adequate. Defensively, the outfield was the best in the league. On the offense, Huggins had massed a terrific attack. The center of it was carried by Ruth, Gehrig, and Meusel.

This trio, thrown together for the first time in 1925, really began to click in 1926. Before the coming of Gehrig, enemy pitchers frequently passed Ruth, preferring to take a chance even on Meusel, and sometimes they got away with it. Now the threat was accentuated. A pitcher couldn't pass Ruth without bringing up Gehrig. And if, somehow, he got past Gehrig, there still was Meusel.

Two stories linger from the era that dawned with the rush of the Yankees to the front that spring.

One day the Yankees were playing the Cleveland

Indians in Cleveland, and Joe Shaute, one of the best pitchers of his time, was in the box for the Indians. Ruth, Gehrig, and Meusel were all right-field hitters, and as there is a short right-field fence at League Park, Shaute pitched outside to them in an effort to make them hit to left field. Ruth hit a line drive that struck Rube Lutzke, the third-baseman, on the shoulder and bowled him over. Gehrig cut his legs from under him with a smash that struck him on the shin. Meusel's drive hit him in the stomach and he went down for the third time. Moreover, he made no move to get up.

The players gathered about him in alarm.

"Are you hurt, Rube?" Shaute asked, anxiously.

"Am I hurt!" the Rube yelled. "Why, a guy would have been safer in the World War!"

Another concerns Grady Adkins, a young pitcher with the Chicago White Sox. Adkins, in his first year in the league, had been going full blast. And then the Yankees moved into Chicago.

"Moe," Adkins said to Moe Berg, then catching for the White Sox, "what about these Yankees? Can they really hit as hard as everybody says?"

Moe, who did not want to frighten the young man, shook his head.

"No," he said. "Pay no attention to anything you hear about the Yankees' power at the plate. It's all newspaper talk. If you pitch today—and I think you will—just get in there and pitch as you would against any other club.

Adkins pitched that day. That is, he pitched for about two innings and then the Yankees, with Ruth, Gehrig, and Meusel in the van, shelled him from the box. As he went down the steps into the dugout on his way to the showers, he glared at Berg, who wasn't catching that day.

"Berg," he said, "I will never believe another word you say. Not as long as you live."

The Yankees rolled through the first half of the 1926 season, piling up a long lead. It was to serve them well as the season lengthened and waned. Possibly because of their eagerness to sew up the race too quickly, they hadn't paced themselves well, and they staggered through the last few weeks and very nearly came upon disaster as, closing out the campaign in the West, they lost four games of a six-game series in Cleveland. But the aging Dutch Ruether, in a magnificent effort, pitched them to victory in the final game, and they left Cleveland with a two-game lead over the Indians and only a few days to go. They clinched the pennant in St. Louis a day or so after the Cardinals had clinched the National League pennant in New York.

The Yankees had come back. From seventh place they had swept to the top in the course of a single season, with a kid at short stop, a kid at second base, and, for that matter, a kid at first base. The kid at first base had hit. 313. His home-run production had fallen off, for he made only sixteen. But nevertheless he had been molded into a powerful attack and hitting in the clean-up spot had driven in 107 runs.

The world series was exciting, with the Cardinals, managed by Rogers Hornsby, winning in seven games. The peak play of the series came in the seventh inning of the last game, played on a dark Sunday afternoon at the Stadium, when Grover Cleveland Alexander, coming in as a relief pitcher with the bases filled, two out, and Lazzeri at bat, struck Tony out.

Gehrig was bitterly disappointed, as were all the Yankees, of course, by their failure to climax the winning of the pennant with a victory in the series. His disappointment could not be lessened by the fact that he was one of the stand-out players in the series, hitting .348 and accepting seventy-nine chances without an error. All that mattered to him was that the Yankees had lost.

In the spring of 1927 the Yankees came hammering back from their defeat in the world series. Huggins had had to make few changes in his team. It had been hardened and tempered under fire in 1926. The three youngsters in the infield—Lou and Lazzeri and Koenig—had settled into their major league stride, and Dugan still was the top third-baseman. Ruth never was greater and never had had two outfielders of the caliber of Combs and Meusel on the picket line with him. The catching was in the capable hands of Johnny Grabowski and Pat Collins. Hoyt, Pennock, and Pipgras were in fine form.

The power of the team at the plate was such that even in the early days of the season it was written that here was a new Murderers' Row, the fearsome tag that had been used to describe the array of hitters that Huggins had marshaled back in 1921, when he had won his first pennant. And then, as the season rolled on, it was seen that this was a better team than that which had ruled the league from 1921 through 1923.

The most important addition to it was Wilcy

Moore, who had knocked around in the minor leagues for several years with no hope of ever getting to the majors and then had been bought by the Yankees out of the South Atlantic League just as, in his own language, he "was fixin' to go home" at the end of the 1926 season and seriously considering staying there, believing his future lay in tilling the rich loam of his Oklahoma farm and not in further scrabbling about on minor league fields. He was a big, quiet, good-natured fellow—and in the estimation of the ball players and critics, the greatest relief pitcher that ever lived. Bill Killefer, coach that year with the St. Louis Browns, voiced the sentiments of all of the Yankees' opponents one day in St. Louis when the Browns, trailing in a late inning, rallied and began to clout the Yankee pitcher. Huggins held up the game and beckoned to Moore, who was in the bullpen, and Killefer, in the Browns' dugout, groaned.

"It's all off boys," he said. "Here comes Frank Merriwell."

The Yankees swept along, battering the enemy into submission. On the Fourth of July the Senators, who had hacked their way into second place and constituted at least a faint threat to the Yankees, moved into the Stadium for a double-header. The Yankees

117

won the first game, 12 to 1—and the second, 21 to 1.

"These fellows not only beat you but they tear your heart out," Joe Judge, Washington first-baseman, said as he was leaving the park after the games. "I wish the season was over."

This was the greatest season Lou had had, one of the greatest he ever was to have. Most of the rough edges had been knocked off his fielding. His hitting was terrific. The rush and clatter of the Yankees, the roar of the crowds at the Stadium, a consciousness of his own growing ability—these thrilled him as nothing ever had done before.

Years before, Larry Doyle had said:

"It's great to be young—and a Giant."

Now Lou must have said to himself over and over again, in one way or another, that it was great to be young and a Yankee. Why, just to move from one town to another with the Yankees was a thrill. The staring crowds in the stations as the long line of cabs bearing the players rolled up, the eager rush of the porters for their luggage, the deference of the railroad agents and the train crews, the poker or bridge games or the quartets on the trains, the arrivals at the next town, the surge of the players into the lobby of the hotel. Gangway! It's the Yankees! And he was not only one of the Yankees but one of the greatest of the Yankees. The slugging first-baseman of a team they said was the greatest that ever had been assembled.

Once they left Boston for Detroit—an unusual jump, since the schedule usually is arranged with a view to making the jumps as short as possible. This time, however, the Yankees left Boston shortly after the game and were not due in Detroit until noon the next day and then, to make matters worse, the train was delayed, the dining car had been taken off after an early breakfast and the players who slept late had eaten nothing when they reached Detroit at three o'clock. There was no time for them to go to the hotel, since three o'clock was the hour at which the game was supposed to start and the crowd already was in the park.

The cabs, with an escort of motorcycle police, raced from the station to the park. The players, tumbling out of the cabs, rushed for the clubhouse, the hungry ones stopping at refreshment booths under the grandstand to grab some food and take it with them to be eaten as they dressed. Hot dogs . . . sandwiches . . . milk . . . pop . . . an assortment of stuff calculated, especially when eaten hurriedly, to give anybody a rollicking attack of indigestion. But it had no such effect on the Yankees. They gulped it down and, waiving both batting and fielding practice, hurled themselves at the Tigers—and flattened them by a score of 19 to 2.

The race virtually had ended with the smashing of the Senators on July 4. From there on, the only remaining doubt concerned the number of games by which the Yankees would win. The pennant was clinched on Labor Day in Boston, and that night on the platform of the Back Bay station, where they were to take the train for New York, Lou and the Babe presided at the ceremonial bonfire built of straw hats grabbed from the heads of the players.

With the pennant clinched, there was no let-down on the part of the Yankees. Winning—and winning by the biggest possible score—still was too much fun. Near the end of the season, Huggins granted permission to the regulars to take themselves out of the line-up at any time when they didn't feel like playing. A few of them took advantage of the offer. Among those who didn't was Lou. What! Miss a day at the ball park, even to go fishing? No, sir. Fishing could wait. And so he rounded out his second complete season by playing in every game. He hit .373, made forty-seven home runs, and drove 175 runs over the plate.

It is rather generally agreed that the Yankees won the world series from the Pirates that year the day before the series opened. And if that sounds fantastic, here is the explanation: the Pirates, having finished their work-out before the Yankees took the field, sat in the stands as the American League champions began their batting practice. It was a sorry mistake, for they saw Ruth, Gehrig, and Meusel step to the plate and smash the ball into the right-field stand, over the left-field fence, and even over the fence in center.

Most of them, at one time or another, had seen Ruth and Meusel. Few, if any, of them ever had seen Lou. And what they saw of him was terrifying for it was he who hit the ball over the center field fence, a feat never performed by any National League hitter, even in batting practice. That demonstration of power was too much for them. They knew, right there, that they couldn't cope with this slamming crew. Nor could they, and the Yankees beat them in four straight games

One of the features of the two games played in Pittsburgh was the amazing fielding of Gehrig under difficult conditions. Field boxes had been built back of first base, cramping Lou's territory but not, as it developed, his style. For what the young man had done on that day of practice before the game was to measure off carefully the distance he could go to his left until, after a few trials, he could have covered it blindfolded. Three times during the two games, as his teammates yelled to him in warning, he caught foul flies at the very edge of the boxes. Once he went right over the low wall of a box as he caught the ball, crashing among the startled occupants—but clinging to the ball.

He had a good series at the bat, too. He hit only .308 and didn't make any home runs, but of his four hits, two were doubles and two were triples, and he hammered five runs across the plate.

The 1928 season was, in large part, a repetition of the season that had gone before. Bad luck attended the Yankees near the end of the campaign when minor injuries caused some of the players, Lou included, to resort to tape and bandages.

"The Yankees," it was written, "are held together by sticking plaster. But even so they are too much the best."

Crowded by the Athletics as the season wore to a finish, they turned savagely on Connie Mack's team, drove it back, rushed on, won the pennant, and then beat the Cardinals in four straight games in the world series.

Lou, who had hit .374 and made twenty-seven home runs during the season, had his greatest world series. Before he had not hit a home run in a series. This time he hit four, two of them in one game. He made five hits in eleven times at bat for an average of .545 and drove in nine runs.

The battered crew had risen in truly great fashion, responsive to the pressure of the series.

"The Yankees," it was written, "won the series on one leg."

10. The Death of Miller Huggins

NOW, for the first time, a cry was raised. A cry that was to be repeated ten years later:

"Break up the Yankees!"

Clearly, there was no team in either league that was a match for them. Something would have to be done to bring them down somewhere near the level of their rivals.

"Ruppert should give the other clubs a break," critics and fans in other cities said. "Why doesn't he sell some of his stars? It would be too much to expect him to sell Ruth, of course. But why doesn't he sell Gehrig or Meusel or some of the others?"

Sell Gehrig? Well, he could have sold him at his own figure. There wasn't a club in the league that could have afforded to buy him that wouldn't have leaped at the chance—and the clubs that couldn't have afforded it would have borrowed the money— and then leaped.

Lou had not yet reached the zenith of his skill as a first-baseman, but he no longer was the awkward fellow he had been when first he had put on a Yankee uniform. He had three full seasons and part of a fourth behind him. And three world series. There were pitchers in the league who frankly confessed they would rather pitch to Ruth than to him. He was twenty-six years old, powerful, tireless, and deceptively fast. The zest for playing the game that he had known as a boy had increased rather than lessened. He still thought that playing a ball game was fun—and that playing a double-header was more fun.

Through the winter of 1928-1929 baseball writers who had nothing else to write about and, it must be confessed, no better sense, speculated on the possibility of the Yankees putting Gehrig on the market, guessed at the price he would bring. Fifty thousand dollars? A hundred thousand? Ruth had brought $100,000, but prices had gone up. This was what Westbrook Pegler has called the "Era of Wonderful Nonsense." Money didn't mean anything because everybody had so much of it—or seemed to have. A hundred and fifty thousand?

It didn't mean anything, of course, since Ruppert had no intention of selling any of his stars, and, if he had, Gehrig certainly would not have been put on the market. But it must have made Lou's head swim sometimes when he read these stories. The Little Dutch Boy, with his patched pants, and his empty pockets, the nobody who did his homework on the streetcars or in the kitchen of the Sigma Nu house, had become somebody. His salary was mounting, he had provided comforts once undreamed of for his father and mother, and he was worth a fortune to the man who employed him—and the man scorned the fortune, preferring him instead.

Huggins, smiling at the cry of "Break up the Yankees!" said:

"It won't happen—and it isn't necessary. Time and the law of averages will take care of that. Ed Barrow will dig up the best ball players he can find, through his scouts, in the colleges and the minor leagues. The Colonel will buy them and they will be turned over to me, and I will develop them and manage them to the best of my ability, and they will try as hard as they can. But in spite of all that, one of these days they will fail. Empires, great private enterprises, and personal fortunes have been broken up by time. Who do these people who have raised this cry think the Yankees are that they can go on forever."

Huggins, sound, wise, far-sighted, said that in the

126

spring of 1929 as the Yankees assembled once more in St. Petersburg for their training. He was right, of course. And yet he could not see that the end of the Yankees' reign was almost at hand or know that never again would he return to the field where he had built this powerful team.

Connie Mack had been progressing steadily in his efforts to win a pennant with the Athletics for the first time since the dissolution of his team that had won four times in five years—in 1910, 1911, 1913, and 1914. Hundreds of players had trooped through the clubhouse in Philadelphia as Connie had brought them in, looked them over—and turned them out. But for four years, now, the A's had been strong contenders, having finished second in 1925, third in 1926, second in 1927 and again in 1928. Lefty Grove, George Earnshaw, Mickey Cochrane, Jimmy Dykes, Al Simmons, Eddie Rommel—they had come with a rush and now they were ready. They wasted little time proving it but went to the front almost as soon as the season opened.

The Yankees promptly set out in pursuit, but as the weeks lengthened into months, their hopes faded. Huggins shook up the team, rearranged his batting order, alternately pleaded with his players and lashed them savagely. There came a day in August when he walked into Ruppert's office in the Stadium after a losing game and said:

"We'd better start getting ready for next year, Colonel."

The Colonel, reluctant to believe his team would not win again, was startled.

"Why, Hug," he said, "we still have six weeks to go, and with all that has happened to us, we are not so far behind."

"That's right," Hug said. "But these fellows are through."

"How do you know?"

"I have just been talking to them," Hug said. "I have been talking to them for twenty minutes. I bawled them out. I called them everything I could think of. I even accused them of quitting—although I know they didn't. And when I got through, nobody said anything. If somebody had called me names . . . if somebody even had laughed . . . I would have felt there still was hope. But they sat there looking at me as though they had no interest in me or what I was saying, and I realized that for twenty minutes I practically had talked to myself. And so, I tell you, they are through."

They were through. They weren't so far back, as Ruppert had said, but they couldn't get up. The team that fans and critics, weary of their success, had wanted broken up, had crumbled—almost overnight, it must have seemed to Huggins. And Huggins was worn and tired and sick. His face, always pinched, was haggard. His thin body had become even thinner.

The Yankees stumbled on, Gehrig stumbling with the rest. Recurrent batting slumps had beaten his average down to about .300. True, there are players who never hit as much as .300 although they may play years in the major leagues, but for Lou it was a low mark, representing a drop of seventy-four points from his final average at the close of the 1928 season.

As a team the Yankees were depressed, and yet the loss of their power was as nothing compared to the loss that they were to suffer. On September 20, Huggins was so ill when he reached the Stadium that he barely could get into uniform. The players and his coaches, Arthur Fletcher and Charlie O'Leary, begged him to go home.

"I'll be all right," he said. "Don't worry about me."

He went out to the dugout, watched the teams at batting practice, and made out the batting order for the umpires. When the game started he was in his usual place, crouched on the dugout steps. But after three innings he had to withdraw. The club physician, called to the clubhouse by the anxious O'Leary, examined him and, finding he had a mounting temperature, bundled him into a taxicab and took him to St. Vincent's Hospital.

"Look after the team while I'm resting for a few days," he said to Fletcher. And then, with a wry smile, "See if you can't do better with it than I have."

When he entered the hospital he was not believed to be seriously ill, but two days later his condition took a grave turn. On September 25, as the Yankees were gathering at the Stadium for the day's game, he died.

The players were numb with grief. Some of the older members of the team—Ruth and Meusel and a few others—had not liked him very much when first they knew him, but they had grown to love him, while the younger players idolized him.

To Lou he had been a friend from the day the boy first walked, awe-struck, into the Yankees' clubhouse. Lou was one of the Little Miller's pallbearers and accompanied the body to Cincinnati, where Hug had been born and reared and where he lies in Wood-lawn Cemetery.

The dwindling days of the season meant nothing to Lou. He didn't care whether he hit the ball or didn't, nor who won or lost a game. For the first time in his life, there was no joy in going to the ball park each day, and the end of the season came as a relief. Now, at least, he would not have to see every day the battered roll-top desk where Hug had sat in the clubhouse, nor miss his crouching figure on the dugout steps.

With the death of Huggins, the Yankees moved into a new phase. Huggins had fulfilled Colonel Ruppert's hopes for a pennant and a world-championship. True, the Colonel, by liberal use of his bankroll, had furnished the players with whom these flags had been won. But Huggins had managed the players better than anybody else Ruppert could have had. He had grown in stature until, at his death, he was rated on a par with John McGraw and Connie Mack as a manager. He was, in short, recognized as one of the greatest managers baseball ever had known. And now he was dead and Ruppert and Barrow looked for his successor.

Their first choice was Donie Bush, who had been managing the Pittsburgh Pirates of the National League, but unknown to them he had just signed a two-year contract to manage the Chicago White Sox. The call then went to Eddie Collins, who had slowed down as a player with the Athletics, but Collins rejected it, preferring to remain with Connie Mack. Now they turned to one who already was in a Yankee uniform—to Arthur Fletcher, who had joined the team in 1927 as a lieutenant under Huggins. Fletcher had learned his baseball under McGraw, subsequently had managed the Phillies, had retired from baseball, and then, after a year, been persuaded by Huggins, who had known him well in the National League, to sign with the Yankees.

Fletcher, quickly adapting himself to his new surroundings, had been of great aid to Huggins. He was popular with the players, he was a sound baseball man, he was aggressive. New York fans had admired him for twenty years. He was a good man for the job. That's what Ruppert and Barrow thought. That was what everybody else thought. Everybody, that is, but Fletcher.

"No," he said, when Ruppert called him into his office. "No, thanks, Colonel. I was happy as a coach under Miller Huggins. I will be happy to serve his successor, whoever he is."

Ruppert and Barrow tried to persuade him to

change his mind. But to no avail. Fletcher had managed the Phillies for five years and had had an untold number of headaches and heartaches. He was independent financially of baseball or any job that it had to offer. He wanted to remain in the game because he loved it. But he did not want to be a manager again. No sum that Ruppert could have offered him could have caused him to change his mind. That day he went back to his hotel and said to Mrs. Fletcher:

"I have just turned down the best job in baseball."

Mrs. Fletcher was happy. She didn't want him to be a manager again.

The fourth choice of Ruppert and Barrow—still looking within their own ranks for a manager—was Bob Shawkey. Shawkey, one of the players purchased from the Red Sox when the Yankees were drawing their strength from Boston, had been a good pitcher and a smart one. He had a fine baseball mind, and the other players liked him. With Fletcher out of the running and with Ruppert and Barrow now determined to put a Yankee at the head of the Yankees, he undoubtedly was the best man they could have picked. Informed of the nomination, Shawkey accepted it.

And so, at St. Petersburg in the spring of 1930, the

Yankees started a new drive under a new manager. Nobody expected Shawkey to win a pennant that year. That would have been too much to have expected anybody to do. The players fell in behind him and did the best they could, but still the team lagged. Shawkey knew he had to make some changes. Older players were wearing out and had to be replaced. He began to make deals. To trade with other American League clubs, to bring players up from the minors. The character of the team changed almost overnight. Still, while the Yankees remained in the running there was no great improvement in them.

"Do you know what is the trouble with this team?" Waite Hoyt asked one night in St. Louis.

And without pausing for an answer, he said:

"There are too many fellows on it who aren't Yankees."

Hoyt has a great gift for words. Those who have heard him on the radio in recent years know that. But he had it then. And he never made a happier choice when he put into ten words the situation in which the Yankees found themselves in 1930. There were too many fellows on the team who weren't Yankees. The Yankees were Ruth and Gehrig and Meusel. And Pennock and Lazzeri and Hoyt and

Dugan. Fellows like that. And now some of them were passing from the scene, and the players who were replacing them weren't Yankees.

And Gehrig? Gehrig was holding up. Better than that. He had recovered from the slumps that had dragged him down in 1929. The shock of Huggins' death, although never to be forgotten, was wearing off. He was slamming the ball in his old style. He was a better first-baseman than he had been. He was not yet the first-baseman that he was to be but he constantly was improving.

The Yankees couldn't win the pennant that year. They couldn't finish second. They wound up in third place behind the Athletics and the Senators. But it was one of Lou's best years. He hit .379, hammered out 41 home runs, and drove in 174 runs. Long recognized as one of the outstanding players of the game, he had achieved stardom.

Ruth still was the acknowledged king, although that year he had hit an even twenty points below Gehrig and had made only eight more home runs. But Gehrig was the crown prince. He walked in the Babe's shadow, as he was to do through all the years that the Babe played in New York. But jealousy of the Babe was entirely missing from his make-up—

jealousy of the Babe or, for that matter, of anybody else. For all the years they had been together—for all the years he had followed the Babe to the plate, frequently stopping to congratulate the Babe on hitting a home run just before hitting one himself—the Babe still was his hero.

So, in 1930, were the Yankees. So was Lou Gehrig.

Eight hundred miles away and in the other league, as the ball players say, forces were at work. Forces that were to affect the destinies of the Yankees . . . and of Lou Gehrig.

11. The Coming of Joe McCarthy

THE manager of the Chicago Cubs at the outset of the 1930 season was Joseph Vincent McCarthy, native of Philadelphia, son of a contractor, who had played cricket in his youth—Joe was born and reared close to the Germantown Cricket Club—and a minor leaguer through all his playing days. He had played with Wilmington in the Tri-State League, with Franklin in the Inter-State League, with Toledo in the American Association, and with Wilkes-Barre in the New York State League. There—that is to say, in Wilkes-Barre—he had had his first experience as a manager, and then he had been sold to Buffalo and then, after two years, he had been sold to Louisville in the American Association. There he had been appointed manager. There he had won pennants in 1921 and 1925. More important, from a major league standpoint, he had developed ball players who were ready made when they came to the major leagues.

And so, when William Wrigley, Jr., who owned the Cubs, was looking about for a manager to supplant George Gibson at the end of the 1925 season, John B. Foster, who had been a baseball writer for many years and then secretary of the Giants and, finally, a baseball writer again and in touch with the baseball set-up all over the country, suggested that he engage McCarthy. Wrigley, acting on the suggestion, conferred with several of his baseball friends in whom he had implicit confidence. They recommended that he sign McCarthy.

McCarthy took over a club that had finished last in 1925. In 1926, it finished fourth. Again in 1927 it finished fourth. In 1928, he landed it in third place. And in 1929, he won the pennant. This was the Cubs' first pennant since 1918, their second since 1910. Chicago was wild about McCarthy. So was Wrigley. But the Cubs lost the world series to the Athletics, four games to one, and Chicago cooled off on McCarthy. So, in 1930, did Wrigley, especially when he saw his team could not repeat. Near the end of the season he dismissed McCarthy, replacing him with Rogers Hornsby.

Just about that time Ruppert and Barrow—and

LOU GEHRIG with COLONEL RUPPERT and JOE McCARTHY

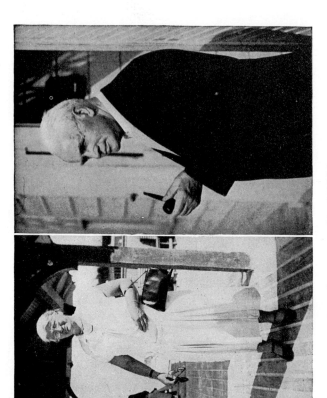

MOM AND POP GEHRIG

A FAMILIAR SCENE: THE BABE AND LOU

© *Boston Herald*

THE 1927 INFIELD: GEHRIG, LAZZERI, KOENIG, DUGAN

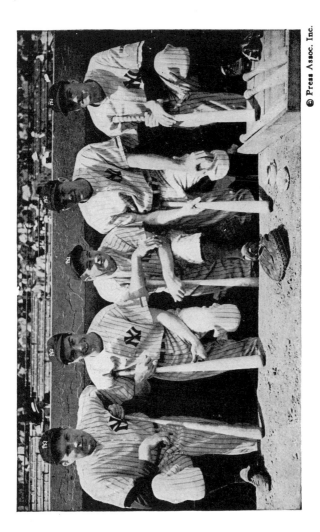

© Press Assoc. Inc.

TEAMMATES IN 1939: RUFFING, DIMAGGIO, GEHRIG, DICKEY, PEARSON

LOU AND ELEANOR

A SMALL BOY LOOKS AT HIS HERO

KEY LARGO: LOU AND BILL DICKEY

their names always must be linked in this phase of the Yankees' history because Ruppert leaned heavily on Barrow and made no move without Barrow's suggestion or support—decided that Shawkey was not the man they wanted to lead the Yankees. The Yankees were winding up in third place—or two places below that in which the Colonel wanted his team to finish—and there was no indication that to continue with him in command would better the status of the team.

Joe Vila, sports editor of the *New York Sun*, had become interested in McCarthy through John Foster, who was writing for his pages. He called Barrow the moment he heard McCarthy was through in Chicago, and Barrow, long an admirer of McCarthy, called Ruppert. The result was an invitation to McCarthy to take over the management of the Yankees. Warren Brown, now of the *Chicago Sun*, but then sports editor of the *Herald-Examiner*, who was as close to McCarthy as Vila and Foster, urged him to accept. McCarthy, whose career as a major league manager had been confined to the National League and who had seen very few American League games, was hesitant. But Vila, Foster, and Brown were obdurate. And so, during the world series that year between the St. Louis Cardinals and the Philadelphia

Athletics, he met Ruppert and Barrow in a Philadelphia hotel and agreed to take the post.

Almost immediately he was assailed by misgivings. He knew, as everybody in baseball knew, that the management of the Yankees had been offered to Fletcher the year before. What he didn't know was that Fletcher, having watched Shawkey manage the team through one season, hadn't changed his mind. Suppose Fletcher had reconsidered and, not having been consulted by Ruppert and Barrow, resented McCarthy's appointment? McCarthy didn't know Fletcher very well. Theirs was but a snarling acquaintance, dating from the time when Fletcher managed the Phillies and, both being out of the old school of baseball, they had fought each other bitterly.

The first thing McCarthy did on his return to his home in Buffalo was to call Fletcher on the telephone at his home in Collinsville, Illinois. Did Fletcher feel slighted that he, McCarthy, had been called over from the National League to manage the Yankees? . . . No. . . . Would Fletcher meet him in Chicago in a few days to talk over the situation and tell him something of the American League, about which he was profoundly ignorant? . . . Yes. With pleasure.

140

And so, a few days later, they got together in Chicago. Fletcher welcomed Joe cordially, assured him of his loyalty, and told him all he could, at that moment, about the league that he would enter with the coming of spring in 1931.

So far, so good. And then, just before the opening of the 1931 season, Ruppert said to his new manager:

"McCarthy, I finished third last year. I realize that you are confronted with problems that it will take you a little while to solve, and so I will be content if you finish second this year. But . . . I warn you . . . I do not like to finish second, I like to win."

"So do I, Colonel," McCarthy said. "I will win this year, if I can. But if I fail, I will win next year, so help me."

Gehrig read with interest of the engagement of McCarthy, whom he did not know. Indeed, it is probable that he never had seen the man.

As a matter of fact, McCarthy was a complete stranger to almost all the Yankees. Earle Combs had played for him in Louisville, and one or two others had a nodding acquaintance with him, but to the rest he was just a name, since players in one major league are not likely to see much of the players and managers in the other except during a world series or spring training, and the paths of the Yankees and Cubs never crossed each other in the spring with the Yankees training in Florida and the Cubs in California.

It was characteristic of Lou that he should have acknowledged McCarthy's authority even without thinking about it; he was a player and McCarthy was the manager. He was prepared to serve Mc-Carthy as faithfully as he had served Huggins and Shawkey. McCarthy knew this. If he hadn't been able to guess it, it was told to him by Fletcher. There was no need for McCarthy to give another thought to this young man, who could be depended upon to play every day, to take excellent care of himself between games, and, on or off the field, to reflect credit on himself and the Yankees.

Unhappily for McCarthy, all the Yankees of the spring of 1931 weren't so constituted and so minded. As Waite Hoyt had said, there were too many fellows on the club who weren't Yankees. They had come in during a period of uncertainty and upheaval, and they already were marked for shipment elsewhere. Meanwhile, they were at St. Petersburg and McCarthy had to concern himself with them.

Besides, there was a very definite anti-McCarthy group of older players. They didn't know McCarthy any better than Gehrig did, and certainly the stories they had heard about him could not have prejudiced them against him. But they resented his presence in command of the team because they thought that Babe Ruth should have been Shawkey's successor. No one openly had nominated the Babe for the job, nor had he expressed any ambition in that direction. But he was the oldest member of the team in point of service and he was the Babe and some of his team-mates thought that Ruppert and Barrow had slighted him by reaching into the National League for a manager.

There were few outward manifestations of this attitude on the part of some of the players. McCarthy quickly established himself as a disciplinarian, played no favorites, whipped the team into shape in a couple of weeks, and then attacked his exhibition schedule. Huggins never had been too intent on winning exhibition games in the spring or even in the summer, for that matter. He regarded the spring games with minor or other major league clubs simply as a part of the conditioning of his players. If the Yankees won them, all right. If they didn't, well, that was all right, too. He was interested only in getting them in shape for the season. Shawkey felt the same way. But not McCarthy.

McCarthy always has wanted to win every game his teams have played, spring, summer, or fall. The first game the Yankees played that spring was with the Milwaukee club of the American Association. Surprised at first by McCarthy's attitude when the game started, the care with which he picked his pitchers, and the vigor with which he urged the players on, they decided to unbend and give him a real victory, since that was what he so obviously wanted. So they tore into the astonished Brewers and beat them by a score of 19 to 1. As they were climbing into the buses to take them from Waterfront Park, where the game had been played, to Huggins Field, where they dressed, Jimmy Reese, the kid second baseman up from the Pacific Coast League, said:

"Well, Joe, how did you like that? Nineteen to one!"

McCarthy scowled.

"Against a team like that," he said, "you should have made thirty runs."

The players looked at one another. A new standard had been set for them. There would be no waiting for the opening bell of the season to set them on their way. They were on their way now.

"You know, Bill," Lou said to his roommate, Bill Dickey, that night, "I like this McCarthy."

"So do I," Bill said. "He's our kind of guy, Lou."

He was—and still is. As the years went on, Gehrig's respect and admiration for McCarthy was to increase —and so was McCarthy's for Gehrig. Joe never has asked for anything from his players save the best they have to offer on the field, and he got that from Lou from the day he took over at St. Petersburg. Later the relationship grew far beyond that of just a manager and a player.

McCarthy was to become, as Huggins had been and Barrow continued to be, a man who had a tremendous influence on Lou's life. There was something about the big, whole-souled young man that attracted McCarthy to him immediately—something that had nothing whatever to do with his ball playing. In short, Lou had the same effect on him that he had on everyone he met, and McCarthy grew to look upon him as he might look upon a son or a younger brother.

145

Within the last year or so Lou really had emerged as a star. As a first-baseman he had no rival in the American League, and only Bill Terry of the Giants in the National. Day after day he was hammering away at the plate. Never missing a game. Hitting singles, doubles, triples, home runs. Driving in runs. In 1930, as the Yankees strove futilely to get back to the top of the league, he hit .379, smashed out forty-one home runs and drove in 174 runs.

Nobody noticed it but he hadn't missed a game since that day, back in 1925, when Huggins sent him in to give Wally Pipp a rest. And now he was swinging up through the South as the spring of 1931 wore on. Hitting all the exhibition towns. Vying with Ruth as a drawing card, vying with him in long smashes as he followed him to the plate. Drawing on to New York and the opening of another season.

But stardom had its worries, too. It had taken him a long time to get up there, starting from the sidewalks, the corner lots, the public parks. Now he had arrived—and he found a new struggle on his hands: the struggle to stay there. He no longer was just a young fellow trying to make good. He was Lou Gehrig, first-baseman of the Yankees. The team that had been the best in baseball . . . and was trying hard to be the best again. There was a new manager in command, a man whose future was at stake, a man he already had learned to like and admire, and whom he must not let down.

He no longer had to worry about his fielding. He had learned to make all the plays that a major league first-baseman must make. To come in on a bunt and make the play at second base, or third, or whirl to throw to the second-baseman covering first. To take a ground ball far to his right and get it into the pitcher's hands in the pitcher's last stride as he raced the runner to the bag. To start and complete a double play, taking a ground ball with a man on first base, getting it to the short stop or second-baseman for a force play . . . and then getting back to first in time to take the return throw. To get pop flies back on the grass in short right field, or twisting fouls near the grandstand. To know when to cut off a throw from right field to the plate and when to let the ball go through.

With characteristic perseverance, he had practiced these plays endlessly until now he could make them almost instinctively. He had learned, too, how to make the most of his height and reach, so that by stretching forward on close plays, with the ball flying

147

at him and the runner pounding down the path, he could save that precious split second that meant the difference between a put-out and a potential run for the enemy.

No, he didn't have to worry about his fielding any more. Nor would you have thought, to see him striding to the plate or hear the pitchers on the other clubs talk about him, did he have to worry about his hitting. But he did. A player's batting average is the measure of his success and it is his meal ticket, because—unless, of course, he is a pitcher—that is what his employer pays off on. And always there were new pitchers coming into the league and the old pitchers constantly were scheming how to keep him from hitting. There were days when they succeeded. Days in which, as the ball players say, he couldn't buy a base hit. In other years, too. And now in this year. This year of 1931.

Gehrig never learned that, as Hank Gowdy had said, a ball player couldn't be good every day. All ball players fret when they are in a batting slump. Gehrig fretted more than most of the others. Worried and fretted and threw his bat down in disgust as he popped out or grounded out. And, through 1931, he was in and out of slumps. At one time he was so worried he couldn't even hit a ball solidly in batting practice, which, naturally, caused him to worry more than ever.

Going back to the dugout one day after he had popped a batting practice pitch over the infield, he begged Herb Pennock to tell him what was the matter with him.

"What am I doing up there?" he asked. "What am I doing that keeps me from hitting?"

Pennock shrugged.

"I don't know," he said.

"Have you been watching me?"

"Yes."

"And you still don't know what I'm doing?"

"No."

Lou stalked disconsolately down the steps on his way to the clubhouse. When he was out of earshot, Pennock said:

"I know what he's doing but I am not going to tell him. He is asking everybody on the ball club what's wrong with him—and everybody is telling him something different. If I told him, it would only add to his confusion. He won't come out of it until he gets so desperate he'll quit worrying."

Which was exactly what happened. A couple of

days later Lou, who had been convinced that he never would get a base hit again, began slamming the ball around the park. And then he wondered why he ever had worried so . . . why he had feared that McCarthy might take him off first base because he had become a drag on the team.

It was a curious year for Lou. His batting average dropped from .379 in 1930 to .314, but when he was hitting he was delivering in the pinches, so that he set a league record by driving in 184 runs as the Yankees wound up in second place. When he was hitting, he was getting distance with his drives. Ruth, who had not failed to lead the league in home runs since that dark season back in 1925, was battering away at the peak again, and Lou was battering right along with him. Now Babe was in front, now Lou. The race ended in a dead heat. When the last game of the season had been played, each had made forty-six home runs.

But wait. Look back. Look back to a day in Washington some weeks before. Lyn Lary, the Yankee short stop, was on second base with two out, and Gehrig hit a towering drive to right center. The ball soared over the fence as Lou trotted down to first base, rounded the bag, rounded second, headed for third. Lary, jogging ahead of him, turned third, started toward the plate—and then suddenly veered off toward the Yankees' dugout. He thought, he said later, the ball had been caught. He was going to get a drink of water before resuming his place in the infield. The players looked at him in amazement. Gehrig had lost track of him . . . thinking he had scored. On Lou jogged and, before anybody quite realized what had happened, he had come down the line from third base and crossed the plate.

Now the Senators were rushing at the umpire, screaming that Lou had passed the runner ahead of him and, therefore, was out. They were right, of course. The umpire declared Lou out, the inning was over. Although he had hit the ball out of the park, he had not made a home run. In the records the blow was scored as a triple.

McCarthy and the other players turned angrily on the hapless Lary. But Lou was quick to defend him.

"He's no more to blame than I am," he said. "If I had kept my head up, I would have seen what happened and waited for him to come back and finish his run before I scored."

Lary felt very bad.

"Forget it," Lou said. "We all pull skulls once in a while. I pull plenty of them myself."

When the heat had died down in the dugout, the Yankees laughed about it. In the grandstand, a raucous voiced rooter boomed:

"Hey! Why don't you fellows sleep at night?"

Now everybody was laughing. But when the final check-up was made on the season it was no laughing matter. That lapse in Washington had cost Lou the home-run championship of the American League and the distinction of leading both leagues, since Chuck Klein of the Phillies had topped the National League sluggers with only thirty-one.

Joe McCarthy had finished second in his first year as manager of the Yankees. He had done well and was acclaimed in the New York newspapers. In Chicago some of the newspapermen, still resentful over his dismissal, reminded William Wrigley that he had outdone his successor, Rogers Hornsby, since the Cubs had finished third.

"All right," Colonel Ruppert said. "All right, McCarthy—for your first year. But remember, McCarthy, I don't like to finish second."

"Neither do I, Colonel," McCarthy said.

And now it was the spring of 1932 and the Yankees were moving up from the South again. McCarthy had made over his team somewhat. There was a new pitcher up from the minors, a kid by the name of Johnny Allen, to join the staff and share the burden with Vernon Gomez, a big winner as a first-year man in 1931, George Pipgras, Charlie Ruffing, Pennock, and Dusty Rhodes, who was to be traded during the season to the Red Sox in a deal that brought Wilcy Moore back to the Yankees. Bill Dickey was challenging Mickey Cochrane of the Athletics for recognition as the league's best catcher. Frankie Crosetti, recruited from the San Francisco club, was battling to take the short-stop post from Lary—and finally won it. The veteran Joe Sewell, in his second year with the club after eleven years in Cleveland, was at third base. Tony Lazzeri, still the league's leading second-baseman, was back at the old stand. Babe Ruth still was in right field and Earle Combs in center. Ben Chapman, converted from the infield to the outfield the year before, was in left. And, of course, at first base was Lou Gehrig.

The trials and disappointments of the year before were behind Lou, all but forgotten in the pleasant months he had spent at home between late September and the day on which he packed his trunk for another spring-training trip—his ninth as a Yankee. This, he felt, was to be a good year.

The other Yankees felt the same way. This was to be their year. The lean years were behind them and they were on their way. The end of the Athletics' domination of the league was in sight. They had won the pennant for the third time in a row in 1931 but they had been beaten by the Cardinals in the world series, when a hitherto almost unknown ball player by the name of Pepper Martin had run rampant and had become famous overnight as the Wild Horse of the Osage.

McCarthy drove them hard that year. Harder than he had driven them the year before. But they liked it because they, too, felt as he did. They didn't like to finish second. They wanted to win.

They smashed and battered at the enemy. Ruth . . . Gehrig . . . Lazzeri . . . Dickey . . . Chapman. Their defense had been tightened. Chapman gave added fire to their attack, leading the league in stolen bases as he swept along from game to game.

On June 3, in Philadelphia, Lou performed one of the greatest feats in the long history of baseball. George Earnshaw was pitching for the Athletics and in the first inning Gehrig hit a home run. Going to bat in the fourth inning, he hit another. He went to bat for the third time in the fifth inning—and hit a third home run.

Connie Mack thought it was about time Earnshaw retired for the afternoon. Gehrig, of course, was delivering the heaviest blows but the Yankees as a team were slamming the pitcher. So Connie waved him out and called Roy Mahaffey in from the bull pen. Connie always liked Mahaffey. He thought he was a pretty smart pitcher.

"Wait, George," he said, as Earnshaw started for the clubhouse. "I want you to see how Mahaffey pitches to Gehrig."

When Gehrig stepped up to the plate in the seventh inning, Mahaffey pitched a high fast ball to him—and he hit it out of the park.

"I see, Connie," Earnshaw said. "May I go now?"

Gehrig had hit four home runs. Only twice before had a man hit four home runs in a single game. Ed Delehanty of the Phillies did it on July 13, 1896, and Bobby Lowe of Boston on May 30, 1894.

And yet that day the note of frustration that so often was to be heard in the hours of his greatest triumphs was heard again. That day, in New York,

John McGraw resigned as manager of the Giants and in the papers and on the radio all over the country the big news was not that Lou had hit four home runs but that the thirty-year term of the colorful and dynamic McGraw had come to an end.

That made much less difference to Lou than it did to his friends, who were chagrined that his bright achievement drew only the secondary notice of the writers and broadcasters. He was happy not so much that he had equaled a record written on the yellowing pages of the game's ancient history but that he had helped to win another game in the Yankees' pennant drive.

And so Lou and the Yankees rolled on, piling up victories, destroying the opposition of the Athletics, and at last they came to the hoped-for climax of the tussle within their own league. They won the flag. Ruppert, who did not like to finish second, had a winner again after three years of waiting. McCarthy, who liked to win as much as he did, had delivered in the second year of his service at the Stadium.

The Cubs, in a great late-season rush under Charlie Grimm, who had supplanted Rogers Hornsby as their manager, had won in the National League, and the Yankees moved to meet them in the world series. In each of their last two series, the Yankes had triumphed in four straight games. McCarthy and the players were determined to do no less. Their drive was hard and their aim was true. They smashed the Cubs—in four games.

Lou had hit .349 that year. In the world series he was terrific, hitting .529 and making three home runs.

12. Romance and Marriage

SOMETHING more important even than a pennant and a world series touched Lou's life in 1932. For the first and only time he fell in love.

Girls had played no part in his life before that. As a small boy they didn't interest him. Later, when he was going to high school and college, he had no time for them. There was too much else to crowd his hours—his home life, his sports, and the work that had to be done. The Gehrigs were not very sociably inclined. When they had a little leisure, which was seldom, they preferred to spend it by themselves, either at home or at a movie or on a picnic or in one of the simpler forms of diversion open to persons of limited means. They lived so much within themselves that they had very few friends and saw those few but seldom.

Commerce High School is a boys' school exclusively, so Lou was not thrown into the company of girls during his school hours. Most of the other boys had girl friends and went to dances and parties, but such affairs had no appeal for Lou. He didn't know how to dance, didn't care if he ever learned and, in his few contacts with girls, was shy and dumb so that the girls didn't care much about him, either. Besides, he had no party clothes and no money to spend. No detail of all this bothered him in the least.

At college it was very much the same. There were girls on the Columbia campus, of course. But Lou was more interested in home runs, three-base hits, forward passes, and rolling blocks. Now and then he was seen with a girl. But not often, and never twice with the same girl. Some of the other boys used to tease him about not having a girl.

"Why," he'd say, "I've got a girl!"

"You have? Who is she?"

"My mother! She's the best girl in the world and the only one I want."

For a long time after he joined the Yankees, his social life was as circumscribed as it had been during his school and college years. His few friends were, for the most part, his old friends. Boys who had gone to high school or college with him—Lincoln Werden, who had gone to both and had become a sports writer on the *Times;* Al McLaughlin, who had played baseball with him at Commerce; Harry Kane, his high-school coach; fellows like that. When they got together it was to go fishing or play cards or take in a show.

Now, too, Lou had more time and all the money he needed to take his mother about. (Both Mr. and Mrs. Gehrig went to the ball game almost every day the Yankees were home, and Pop was very critical of Lou, sometimes, although Mom never was, believing Lou never could do anything wrong even when, as it had to be once in a while, he blew a game by striking out or booting a ball in a pinch.) Pop didn't care much about going out. Mom didn't, either, at first. But Lou finally got her. He took her to the best shows and the best restaurants. When the Yankees went to St. Petersburg in the spring, Mom went, too. Pop—of his own accord, of course—stayed home to mind the house and the pets, which ranged from a snapping turtle to a police dog.

As a major league star, Lou—ungallant as this may sound—could not always escape so easily. Young, handsome, famous, there was much about him to attract the susceptible girls not only in New York but in the other cities on the American League circuit and in many places in between. One spring in St. Petersburg, for instance, there was a wealthy woman with a daughter and a yacht. The girl liked Lou. So did the mother. In fact, the mother not only threw the girl at Lou but acted as if she would throw in the yacht, too, if Lou took the daughter. There wasn't anything the matter with the daughter, either. She was pretty, graceful, charming.

The way it is at resort hotels, everybody knows what is happening to everybody else. And so everybody was watching the situation. There came a night ... and a dinner party ... and the headwaiter went to Lou just before the company went into dinner and said:

"I am seating your mother on your left. I have reserved the place on your right for ... ahem ... the young lady."

"I already have reserved the place on my right myself," Lou said. "It is for Mrs. Whipp, a friend of my mother's."

Mrs. Whipp, mother-in-law of a baseball writer covering the camp and a companion of Mrs. Gehrig's on the beach every day, sat on Lou's right. The young lady sat across the table ... and near the other end.

But in the fall of 1932, when the Yankees were in Chicago playing the world series, it happened. There was a little dinner at a friend's apartment the night before the first game at Wrigley Field (there was an open date between the second game in New York, where the series had opened, and the first in Chicago) and there Lou met Eleanor Twitchell. Not for the first time.

"Although he thought so," Eleanor said, long afterward. "He didn't remember the first time. That was in 1928. That night there was rather a large party and, so far as Lou was concerned, I was just one of a number of girls present. I'm sure he didn't even catch my name when we were introduced. He paid no attention to me, not even knowing who I was—or caring. But, of course, I knew who he was. He was Lou Gehrig, the big baseball hero. Besides, I thought he was a very nice young man and, may I say, a very nice-looking one. But very shy, and spent most of the evening talking to the men.

"He was the first major league ball player I ever met and, naturally, I was interested in his career because he was such a famous one and I followed it closely, so that by the time we met again in 1932 I felt that I really knew him because I knew so much

162

about him. He always swore, later on, that he remembered me from 1928, but I'm sure he didn't and I used to tease him about it."

Whether he remembered her or not, he liked her very much. He saw her again while the Yankees were in Chicago and wrote to her as soon as he returned to New York. The friendship ripened quickly into a courtship. The young man who never had been interested in girls was interested in one now. Slender, honey-haired, blue-eyed, pert little Eleanor Grace Twitchell had done something to his heart.

He went to Chicago to visit her family. She went to New York to visit his.

"Mom," Lou said one night.

"Yes?"

"I'm going to marry Eleanor."

Mrs. Gehrig nodded.

"I know," she said. "I knew from the start."

"Not jealous, are you, Mom?" he asked, laughing.

"No," she said, "I will miss you . . . from our house . . . because we have been together so much . . . and you have been such a good son. But it is right you should be married and have a home now of your own. And Eleanor is a lovely girl, and I know you will be so happy with her."

Just then Mr. Gehrig came in.

"Papa," Mrs. Gehrig said, "Lou is going to marry Eleanor."

Pop grinned.

"See?" he said. "What did I tell you?"

Lou and Eleanor were married in New Rochelle on September 29, 1933. The ceremony was performed by the Mayor, Walter G. C. Otto. The scene of the wedding was the apartment where the couple were to live, not far from the home Lou had bought for his parents.

The Yankees were astonished. They had greeted the announcement of the engagement with skepticism. Now he was actually married they still could scarcely believe it.

13. Lou Maintains His Record

ALONG about the Fourth of July in 1933 the Yankees were in Washington, and Dan Daniel of the *World-Telegram*, who has accompanied the Yankees on most of their trips for many years, was coming out of the dining room after breakfast and met Lou, who was seated in the lobby.

"Lou," he asked, "when did you last miss a ball game?"

"Why," Lou said, "I've never missed one. I mean, not since the day I took Wally Pipp's place . . . by the way, Dan, did you ever hear the story about that?"

"Well, I know that Wally hadn't been going very well and Hug wanted to give him a rest for a few days or something like that," Dan said. "What story do you mean? Was there anything else?"

"No, not really," Lou said. "It's only in the way

165

Wally tells it. Of course, I didn't know anything about it at the time. All I knew was that Hug told me I was going to play and I got my mitt and went out there and played. But a couple of years later, Wally told me just what was said between him and Hug. He said that an old injury around the right eye bothered him every once in a while and sometimes the pain would be so great he hardly could see out of the eye, and this day it was giving him the devil and he said to Hug:

" 'Hug, I got a terrible headache. I can hardly see.'

"And Hug said: 'Well, why don't you take the day off? Take a couple of aspirins and lie down, and I'll let Gehrig play today.' "

Lou howled at the recollection of Pipp's subsequent comment.

" 'Take a couple of aspirins for my headache!' he says to me. 'Hug didn't know what a headache you were going to be to me. Why, you big bum,' he says, 'there isn't enough aspirin in the world to cure that headache.' "

"He never got back on first base, did he?" Dan asked.

"No. He had to go to Cincinnati to find a place to play."

166

"And you haven't missed a game?"

"No."

Dan grinned at him.

"Well, you big lug," he said, "I know that as well as you do. The reason I brought it up is this: Do you know how many games you have played in a row."

Lou shook his head.

"No, I don't, Dan. Come to think of it, it must run up in the hundreds somewhere. I just never—"

"Yes," Dan said, "it is well up in the hundreds. I haven't made an accurate check on it, but I will do so. Roughly, it's about 1,250. And do you realize that Scotty's record is only 1,307—and that you will break that record before this season is over?"

Lou was amazed.

"Gosh!" he said. "Why, I never thought of that. . . . I had no idea. . . . But you must be right, Dan. Let's see . . . 1925 . . . 1926 . . . and this is 1933. Why, I sure must be up around there somewhere."

"Certainly you are," Dan said. "When I said I hadn't made an accurate check, I meant it's either 1,250 or 1,251. That's what I'm in doubt about. You remember, of course, the day you first took over the job."

"Yes," Lou said. "June 2, 1925."

"That's right," Dan said. "But didn't you finish out the game the day before?"

Lou shook his head.

"I don't remember," he said. "I know I did finish a game just before I got in there regularly, but whether it was the day before or the day before that, I just can't recall."

"Neither can I," Dan said. "But I have wired the office and I'll know when I get to the ball park, because they're going to wire me there. But anyway, with or without that added game, you're on your way to a record. I just thought you'd like to know."

"I certainly do like to know. That shows how stupid I am. I should have known it before."

"Stupid?" Dan said. "No. You're not stupid. It's just characteristic of you not to think about yourself. Besides, what good would it have done me if you had thought of it? You wouldn't have told anybody about it."

And then Dan, who sometimes affects a hard-boiled manner although there really is nothing hard-boiled about him, said:

"What do you play ball every day for, anyhow? Why don't you take a day off once in a while?"

"Well, I—"

"Wait a minute. I was going to say don't take a day off until you have broken this record. I don't give a damn about your record, really, but I don't want you to spoil my story. Now go ahead."

"All right," Lou said, laughing. "Now I'll tell you."

And now he was serious.

"I guess it's . . . well . . . just like me, Dan," he said. "The way I've always been and, I guess, the way I'll always be. I remember once, when I was a kid in grammar school, I had the grippe or something. Anyway, this morning when I woke up I had a temperature, and my mother began to fix me up and said I would have to stay in bed. That was before my father became an invalid and he had gone off to work, but my mother had to go out and work for a couple of hours in the morning, too, so after she got me settled she said:

" 'Now, you stay right there and I will be back as soon as I can.'

"But I couldn't stay there, Dan. I never had missed a day in school and I felt I just had to be there. So, a little while after my mother left, I got up and dressed and hustled to school. Of course, when she got home and found I wasn't there she was worried— I hadn't had sense enough to leave a note for her—

and she looked around for me and couldn't find me and one of the neighbors told her she had seen me going out with my books. So my mother rushed around to the school and there I was in my classroom. She told the teacher I was sick and the teacher took a good look at me and saw she was right, and they asked me why I had come to school. And I said:

" 'This is where I belong.'

"And my mother says:

" 'Is that so, young man? Well, you belong in bed and that's where you're going.'

"I protested that I didn't want to go home but the teacher said:

" 'Your mother is right, Lou. Go home. And don't worry about being marked absent from school because you have been here and I am going to mark you present.'

"I began to feel better already," Lou said. "I went home with my mother and went right back to bed and took a lot of medicine, and the next morning I was all right and could go to school. So, when you ask me about playing ball every day . . . well, that's the way I am, Dan."

"Very illuminating," Dan said. "I'll let you know about that record tonight."

That night, at dinner, Dan stopped at Lou's table.

"That's right about that game of the day before," he said. "And now, counting today's game, you're up to 1,252."

The stories out of Washington that night—for Dan, thoughtful as always, had given it to the other newspapermen with the Yankees—were the first intimation, curiously enough, that Lou was moving close to a record. So close that he would break it before the season was out. Everybody had taken him for granted so long that nobody but Dan had stopped to count the number of games he had played.

He moved on, smashed the record, hit .334, hit thirty-two home runs, added to his fame—and was unhappy because the Yankees did not win the pennant. They finished second as the Senators, in their first season under the management of the boyish Joe Cronin, crashed through.

The Yankees were playing the Tigers in Detroit. The date was July 13, 1934. Mark it well.

Lou, first man up in the second inning, singled to center. As he ran to first base he suddenly doubled over and seemed about to fall but managed to reach the bag. He was unable to straighten up, and Earle

171

Combs, coaching at first base, calling time, said to him:

"What's the matter, Lou? Did you pull a muscle?"

Lou, obviously in considerable pain, shook his head.

"No," he said. "I think I must have caught cold in my back. It bothered me a little bit last night and again this morning, but this is the first I have felt it since I came out to the park."

Arthur Fletcher had come over from the third base coaching line, and McCarthy and the players in the dugout were peering at Lou anxiously.

"What's the matter?" Fletcher asked.

"A cold in his back or something," Combs said. "Maybe lumbago. You're getting old, Lou."

Even in pain, Lou grinned. It long had been a gag among the Yankees that Combs, whose hair was silvered even when he came up from the minors to join the Yankees, was the oldest man in baseball.

"Why, you old buzzard!" he said. "Lumbago! You ought to know all about that. I'm just a young fellow. I've just caught cold in the muscles of my back. . . . All right, boys. Let's get on with the game."

When play was resumed, Lou edged a few feet off the bag but still couldn't straighten himself, and it was with difficulty that he reached second base when Ben Chapman singled to right. Bill Dickey followed with a line drive to Jo Jo White in center field, and Gehrig, who had started for third base, was unable to reverse himself and so was doubled up on White's throw to Charlie Rogell, the Tiger short stop.

He walked slowly to the dugout.

"How do you feel?" McCarthy asked.

"Pretty good, Joe. I'll be able to go on after I've rested for a minute or so."

When the Yankees had been retired and had gone into the field again, Lou took up his position at first base, but after Rogell, leading off for the Tigers, had popped to Frankie Crosetti, Lou signed that he was through for the afternoon. Doc Painter, the Yankees' trainer, took him to the clubhouse and worked on him, but skilled as Doc is, the pain and discomfort did not lessen. Lou remained on the rubbing table, resting, for the balance of the afternoon, and then went back to the hotel with the other ball players.

That night Painter was with him constantly, trying, by means of heat treatment and massage, to alleviate his distress but succeeding scarcely at all. Lou dropped off to sleep as dawn came on but he awoke to another day of pain. Resolutely, he went out to the ball park and got into his uniform, but when he tried to take batting practice, he realized that he would be unable to play nine innings.

Conscious now of his consecutive game streak and unwilling to have it snapped, he asked a favor of McCarthy—one of the few he ever asked of anyone, although in his lifetime he extended favors to many.

"Joe," he said, as McCarthy came into the dugout, "I won't be able to go the route today, but I'd like to keep that record of mine unbroken because I am sure I will be able to play tomorrow. So I wish you'd do something for me."

"Gladly," Joe said. "What is it?"

"Well, since Crosetti leads off, put me in the batting order as short stop and I'll take one time at bat, so that the record will show that I actually played in the game. Then I'll get out and Frankie, of course, will take his usual place. O. K.?"

"Certainly," McCarthy said.

Curiously enough, McCarthy discovered, Crosetti wasn't feeling well that day, either, so Red Rolfe was assigned to play short stop after Gehrig had retired. Lou dragged himself up to the plate and, although unable to take a full swing at the first pitch, got a piece of the ball, as the ball players say, and singled to right. He jogged painfully down the line, touched first base and then withdrew, Rolfe being put on to run for him and then going to short stop when the Yankees took the field.

It was, of course, the baseball story of the day. Lou Gehrig, suffering from a cold in the muscles or his back . . . or lumbago . . . or something . . . had preserved his record by taking a time at bat and then withdrawing. Moreover, it was the first time his name had appeared in the Yankee batting order in a championship game save as that of the first-baseman. It was a good story. And then Gehrig returned to the line-up the following day and it was forgotten. The streak had been uninterrupted and was growing longer, day by day, and so . . .

But one baseball writer remembered, when Gehrig had died.

"This," James M. Kahn wrote in the *New York Sun*, "was Gehrig's closest escape from having his endurance mark broken, and it is given in detail because it may hold an additional interest for medical men. These attacks occurred occasionally and escaped accurate diagnosis, invariably doubling him over and making it painful and difficult for him to breathe until they wore off in a couple of days. For convenience in reporting them and because of the absence of anything more definite, the sports writers referred to the attacks as lumbago. Gehrig became quite sensitive to the curiosity of the reporters after a while when these attacks hit him, which they did three or four times over a period of four or five years."

Lumbago that July day in Detroit . . . a cold in the muscles of the back . . . or the dread disease that was to take his life in less than six years?

That, on the record, was a great year for Lou—1934. He hit .363 and made forty-nine home runs. He still was moving up, still acquiring skill as a ball player, still gaining in popularity with crowds around the American League circuit. And Babe Ruth . . . his teammate . . . his hero . . . was fading fast. The Babe hit only .288 that year and made only twenty-two home runs. For years they had slugged it out together, rivals in the race for home-run hitting honors from April to late September. "Home Run Derbies," the baseball writers had called these contests. And now they were over. The Babe had fallen back. Lou still was coming on. Although neither of them suspected it the day the season ended, they had played together in a championship game for the last time.

They took a trip that fall and winter, Lou and the Babe. It began as a baseball tour of the Orient and ended in a jaunt around the world, although most of the way after leaving the Orient they did not travel together, each, with his wife, going his separate way.

On his return to New York, the Babe received a provisional contract from the Yankees. He not only was fast wearing out as a player but he and Joe McCarthy did not get on well together, and Colonel Ruppert was sure of neither his physical ability to play 154 games nor his mental slant toward another season under McCarthy. Under the terms of the contract offered to him, he had to prove himself before a definite salary would be set for him. The Babe rebelled at this, and while the rebellion was in progress Emil Fuchs, president of the Boston Braves, stepped in. He wanted the Babe in Boston not only as a player but as a lieutenant to Bill McKechnie, then managing the Braves. This, as both sides saw, was a way out. The Yankees got waivers on the Babe from all the other American League clubs and the Babe went to Boston.

This meant that at last the shadow of the Babe had been withdrawn and Lou stood alone as the head man of the Yankees. There had been no personal rivalry between them. The Babe was made for the floodlights. Lou, to the best of his ability, consistently dodged them and never felt the slightest pang of jealousy because they beat so steadily on the Babe. But surely he had earned the spot in which he now found himself. Hand over hand, through solid years of hard training and unremitting toil on the diamond, he had reached the peak of the Yankee heap. And to emphasize his position, McCarthy conferred upon him the rank of captain of the team, a distinction no other Yankee had known for ten years.

There were those who, even when he was at the training camp at St. Petersburg in the spring of 1935, urged him, in person or by mail, to assert himself.

"Now is your chance," they said. "Ruth has overshadowed you for a long time. Get out there now and show them you have personality and color of your own. Get out there and do the things he did because . . ."

But his real friends were wiser, and his wife, Eleanor, wisest of all. Because she knew he would listen to her above all others, she wrote him a letter

178

filled with love and tenderness and the soundest of advice.

"Be yourself," she wrote, in closing. "The Babe is one fellow and you are another and you never can be like him. Don't try. Just go on being as you are—fine and true and simple—and great in your own right."

And so, through all the days that were left to him as a ball player and in the days beyond that, he was himself and he was great in his own right.

Lou hit .329 in 1935, made thirty home runs and took on added luster as a first-baseman. Nobody remembered now his sometimes clumsy beginning as a major league first-baseman. His only rival as a first-sacker still was Bill Terry, playing manager of the Giants. In New York, Yankee and Giant fans argued heatedly as to which was the better. The argument never was settled to the satisfaction of either group, of course. But they undoubtedly were linked at the top of the field and the others were, so to speak, nowhere.

In 1936, a new hero was tucked into the Yankee line-up—a new glamour guy to take some of the spotlight away from Lou. A young outfielder by the name of Joseph Paul DiMaggio, up from the San Francisco club of the Pacific Coast League. McCarthy was rebuilding again. Some of the players who had won for him in 1932 long since had vanished. He was molding a new team to regain the heights he had stormed so dramatically and lost as swiftly as he had gained them.

Now the crowds were yelling for DiMaggio, the flaming young Italian, and Joe was in there pounding the ball and playing a great game in the field. He had a remarkable record for a first-year man, hitting .329, making twenty-nine home runs and driving in 125 runs as the Yankees rushed to the pennant. But when the final check-up was made, Lou had hit .354, made forty-nine home runs and driven in 152 runs. Once more he had been the big gun in the Yankee attack.

And, once more, in the world series with the Giants that fall, which the Yankees won in six games, he applied the crusher to the enemy's hopes, for while his batting average was only .292, his hits included a double and two home runs and he drove seven runs across the plate.

He still was zooming in 1937. A batting average of .351. Thirty-seven home runs. One hundred and fifty-nine runs driven in. Taking part in every game in spite of bruises that would have kept another player on the shelf, of days when colds wracked his chest and made it difficult for him to breathe clearly . . . days when his back ached him and it was written on the sports pages that his lumbago was bothering him again. Again the Yankees won the pennant. Again they smashed the Giants in the world series. Again Gehrig was in there driving and hammering.

14. The Shadows Lengthen

NOW it was February of 1938 and Gehrig was packing his trunk for another trip to the training camp. This would be his fifteenth. As he hung his suits on the hangers, folded the rest of his stuff, and placed it carefully in the drawers, he must have thought of that first trip, when he went South with little more than he had on his back, and only twelve dollars in his pocket, and he and Benny Bengough had thought to swell their slender funds by working nights as waiters in a New Orleans restaurant.

He was little known then. Young and strong and eager . . . and poverty-ridden. Now, still young, still strong, he was rich and famous the world over and recently had signed a contract for $39,000 for the season. Those days were long ago, the teammates of those days far away. But he still was up there, still moving briskly. And he could look back on an amazing record. Thumping batting averages in regular season and world series games. Home runs that had mounted into the hundreds. Four home runs in one game. Fielding records that might stand for years. And, rising above all, his record for playing in consecutive games.

That was something to be proud of. Funny he never had thought about it until that day in Washington when Dan Daniel had called it to his attention. But he had guarded it carefully since then. There had been days when it seemed it must be broken. The day he was playing an exhibition game in Norfolk and was hit in the head with a pitched ball and carried unconscious from the field. But he had come back the next day in Washington. The day in Detroit when that pain in the back had caught him so terribly for the first time. That really had been a close call. But he had beaten down or got around all the obstacles in his path. He hadn't missed a game. Exhibition game . . . regular game . . . world series game—and how about that all-star game record? He had been in every game, beginning in 1933 when Arch Ward first dreamed it up in Chicago and it was played as part of the big show at the World's Fair.

And now he was off again. When he got to Florida he would run down to Key Largo for a few days of deep-sea fishing. Then up to St. Petersburg and taking it easy there for a few more days, cutting up old touches with Al Lang and Johnny Lodwick and all his old friends in the town. And then there would be that first day at Huggins Field. The wooden clubhouse, with the long dressing room and the pot-bellied stove at one end and Joe McCarthy's office. And the ball players, whom he hadn't seen since last October, trooping in. Gomez and Ruffing and Combs, the Gray Eagle. And Fletch and Johnny Murphy and Lazzeri—no. Tony wouldn't be there. Tony had been released by the Yankees so that he could sign with the Cubs. Phil Wrigley, trying to build up a championship ball club, knew how important spirit was, and he had wanted Lazzeri because Lazzeri had the spirit and maybe he could impart it to the Cubs. Well, Wrigley was right. But Lou would miss Tony. So would all the rest of the Yankees.

Joe Gordon was coming up to take Tony's place. Gordon must be quite a ball player. Lou had been talking to Oscar Vitt, the manager of the Newark club, the season before, and Oscar had said that Gordon was going to be the greatest second-baseman of all time.

And Crosetti would be there and George Selkirk and DiMaggio and Bill Dickey, of whom he was fondest of all. Dickey was his roommate on the road during the season. Had been for some years. Nobody ever had a better roommate—or a better friend.

And there would be the long days in the sun, limbering up, hitting the ball, running the bases, working out at his position. The exhibition games at Waterfront Park and around Florida at the training camps of the other clubs. And then the two weeks tour to New York, playing the Dodgers along the way. And finally, the Stadium once more and the start of another season.

He never had known a greater or more complete happiness. All that he could have asked from the most benevolent fate was his. His wife, his mother and father, his job, his fame, his comparative wealth, his health.

And yet, that day as he packed his trunk, the shadows were beginning to close about him. Never again was he to look forward so confidently to another season. Never again was he to know the complete happiness he knew that day.

There was no hint of this when the season opened. Although the Yankees had won two pennants and two world series in succession, they had lost no whit of their ambition or their drive. McCarthy was demanding a third pennant and they were going to give it to him. They were filled, too, with a new pride. Critics had begun to compare them to the Yankees of 1927, and they wanted to demonstrate that the critics were right.

They got off to a fine start, and Lou got off with them. They rolled on, crushing the enemy, piling up base hits, home runs, victories. Gordon, after a slow start, had found himself at second base. He and Crosetti, at short, made the best second-base combination the Yankees had known in a long time. Red Rolfe was pegging and banging away at third base. In the outfield, DiMaggio was flanked by Selkirk and Tommy Henrich, with Jake Powell for utility duty on the picket line. Bill Dickey still was the best catcher in either league. The pitchers—Ruffing, Gomez, Spurgeon Chandler, Bump Hadley, Johnny Murphy, Steve Sundra, and Monte Pearson—were swinging along.

Nothing could stop them. Nothing could so much as slow them down. But as the season passed the halfway mark and the Yankees moved briskly toward September and another pennant, Gehrig suddenly reeled into a disastrous slump. He called up a memory of all the things Paul Krichell had said to him when he was a kid struggling through the 1923 season at Hartford. He called on all the resources he had built up through his long experience. The slump lingered and grew.

Now and then he would have a day when he seemed himself. He would get two . . . three . . . four hits. Hit one into the stands or over the fence. He would think the slump was over. And then the next day he would be helpless again. He would fling his bat from him in disgust, rage at himself as he clumped back to the dugout.

"Cheer up," one of the other players would say. "You'll come out of it."

But nobody could cheer him up. He took on a haggard look. McCarthy watched him closely, trying to see what he was doing at the plate that was causing his rapid decline in hitting but could see no hitch in his swing, no fault with his stance.

One day near the end of the season, after a game at the Stadium, Toots Shor, the restaurant keeper, Arthur Brown, nightclub master of ceremonies, and Jay Flippen, comedian—all Yankee fans, friends of the players, and daily patrons of the games—were riding downtown in a cab with Jim Kahn. They were talking about Lou and one of them said he was afraid Lou was through as a big-leaguer and another said it looked as though his years of ceaseless play finally were taking their toll of him. Kahn hadn't said anything and Shor turned to him.

"What do you think, Jim?" he asked.

"I think there is something wrong with him," Jim said. "Physically wrong, I mean. I don't know what it is. I haven't any idea. But I am satisfied that it goes far beyond his ball playing. I have seen ball players 'go' overnight, as Gehrig seems to have done. But they simply were washed up as ball players. It's something deeper than that in this case, though."

"What makes you think so?" Toots asked.

"This," Jim said. "I have watched him very closely and this is what I have seen: I have seen him time a ball perfectly, swing on it as hard as he can, meet it squarely—and drive a soft, looping fly over the infield. In other words, for some reason that I do not know, his old power isn't there. That's the reason he isn't getting base hits. He isn't popping the ball into the air or hitting it into the dirt or striking out. He is meeting the ball, time after time, and it isn't going anywhere."

The season rolled on. The Yankees won the pen-

nant. Gehrig finished the season with a batting average of .295. It was the first time since 1925 that he
had failed to hit .300 or better. That he hit as much
as .295 and that he made as many as twenty-nine
home runs was due to the fine start he had made.

In the world series, as the Yankees beat the Cubs
in four straight games, thus becoming the first club
in history to win three series in a row, Lou hit .286,
making four hits in fourteen times at bat. But his
power, as Jim Kahn had seen so clearly, had waned.
He made no doubles, no triples, and no home runs.
His four hits were looping singles.

The winter of 1938-39—outwardly—was a happy
one for Lou. The Yankees had won the pennant again
and the world series in four games and were being
hailed as one of the great teams of all time and he
was the captain of the team and now the season and
the series were over and he was home with Eleanor.
And in the flush of the Yankees' victory there was
public forgetfulness of the fact that he had had a
terrific slump through the last half of the season and
that he had not made an extra base hit during the
world series.

Two pictures of him that winter come clearly to

mind. The setting of one was a dinner given by the Young Men's Board of Trade. Of the other, Joe McCarthy's room at the Commodore the night of the Baseball Writers' dinner.

The Young Men's Board of Trade is, as its name indicates, a group of youthful businessmen in New York and an influential body in molding public opinion. Each year, after careful deliberation, it chooses the young man who, not alone by his work but by his character as well, has set the finest example for the other young men of the community. The year before it had given its accolade to Thomas E. Dewey, energetic gang-busting District Attorney, who had sent half New York's more notorious hoodlums to prison or the electric chair and driven the other half, terror-stricken, into flight. Never before had it looked to the world of sports for its outstanding "Young Man of Manhattan." But this year, to no one's surprise and to everyone's gratification, it had selected Lou.

The dinner at which the formal award was made was held in the Harvard Club of New York. On the dais were many of the town's outstanding citizens, including Dean Hawkes of Columbia, who had known Lou as a youngster on the campus and had followed his career with interest. One after another, they got up and spoke of Lou in glowing terms, and it was significant that they passed lightly over his achievements as a ball player. They were there to talk about him not as a ball player but as a man. A young man still. But a man who had come out of nowhere to show the other young men of the great city what could be done in any field by courage and strength of character and an adherence to the ideals that had been inculcated in him as a youth.

At last it was Lou's turn to speak, and there never was a more self-conscious or bewildered speaker on any dais. It was plain to those who listened to him that he could not grasp the reason for the honor that was being paid to him nor realize that these earnest young men, in honoring him, were honoring themselves. He stumbled through his speech, for he knew not what to say. And yet, stumbling, he was more effective than he would have been had he prepared his speech, because those who listened knew that his words came from his heart.

It was a fine thing, this dinner. It was one of the high spots of his crowded life. It was a tribute paid to him by other worth-while young men who were not merely baseball fans but who had looked upon the work he was doing and the way in which he did it and valued it because he had given so much to the life of the community to which their lives were so firmly bound.

Less formal but equally memorable was the gathering in McCarthy's room after the Baseball Writers' dinner on a night early in February of 1939. The dinner, held annually, gathers together the great and the near great of baseball. The entertainment consists of skits and speeches in which the great and the near great are lampooned and everybody has a hilarious time, and then, when the dinner is over, the crowd breaks up into groups in rooms upstairs where everybody sits around talking, not only about the dinner but about the season just passed and the season just ahead.

This night McCarthy's room—or, rather, his suite of rooms—was jammed. Club owners . . . ball players . . . baseball writers . . . prominent fans. Men whose names were in the headlines and whose pictures were in the papers. Doors opening and closing and men going in and out. McCarthy . . . Ed Barrow . . . George Weiss, head of the Yankee farm system . . . Casey Stengel . . . Burleigh Grimes . . . Al Schacht . . . Waite Hoyt . . . Johnny Vander Meer

. . . Carl Hubbell . . . Billy Terry . . . Eddie Brannick . . . Horace Stoneham . . . Ford Frick . . . Will Harridge . . . Bill Brandt . . . baseball writers whose by-lines were known from coast to coast.

But, somehow dominating the gathering, Lou Gehrig. Sitting on the arm of an easy chair. A handsome guy if there ever was one. In a dinner jacket, his pipe in his mouth, his wavy hair greying at the temples. Taking a full part in the conversation, laughing at the things that were said by the others, recounting tales out of his own experience. The picture of health and of confidence. The Little Dutch Boy grown up.

Yet what thoughts must have lurked behind his poise and his ready humor. Crowded back for the moment by the spell of the gathering on this pleasant and carefree occasion. But there, nevertheless. Rankling within him, tearing at his nerves. Reminding him of the drab days as the season ended, of his comparative failure in the world series. Warning him of the days that lay ahead.

Is it too much to believe that those thoughts were there? Probably not. They were in the mind of Ed Barrow. They must have been. Witness the contract submitted to Gehrig a few days later—and signed by him without a murmur of protest. Barrow was Lou's friend and loved him as though Lou had been his son. But Barrow also owed a duty to the Yankees. And Barrow, looking back on the season of 1938 and ahead to the season of 1939, wasn't certain of Lou. He had seen what had happened to him and was fearful that this, for some reason on which he could not put his finger, was the beginning of the end. And so the contract he drew for Lou in February of 1939 called for a reduction of $3,000 in salary.

This was the first, and the only, time in his life that he had had his salary cut. He admitted the reasonableness of it. Admitted that in 1938 he had not played his accustomed part in the ascendency of the Yankees. It would have been foreign to his nature to have done otherwise.

But, he said, he would prove, in the forthcoming season, that he was himself again.

"I tired in midseason last year," he said. "I don't know why. But I just couldn't get going again."

There was the recurrent question:

"Do you think you have overdone it by playing every day? Don't you think that if you took a few days off once in a while—"

He cut his questioner short.

194

"No," he said.

"Remember what the Babe said."

Lou laughed.

"I remember," he said. "He thought I should take a few days off and go fishing when I felt the strain was wearing me down. Well, the strain hasn't got me yet. And can you imagine me fishing when the Yankees are playing ball?"

"Then you have no doubts about yourself this year?"

"None at all," he said. "Why should I? What are you talking about? I'm still a young fellow, even if I have been around in baseball for a long time. I just had a bad year last year. Anybody can have a bad year. This year I'll make them forget about what happened in 1938."

Wishful thinking? Courage in the face of adversity?

15. Retirement in 1939

NOW it is the early spring of 1939, and this appears in a New York newspaper. The date is March 20th and the writer is in New York:

"The young men covering the Yankees at St. Petersburg are looking with interest and apprehension at Lou Gehrig. Anyone who put a space rule on the dispatches that come out of the camp probably would discover more space has been devoted to Lou than to any of the other players and most of the stories about him have been fearful, pessimistic—and sympathetic.

"Most of the baseball writers obviously feel that if this is not the end for Lou, it is at least the beginning of the end. They do not find it pleasant to chronicle it because Lou has been a great and popular figure for fourteen years and it is not an easy thing for

them to write anything that may seem to be knocking the props from under him as he tries to hold his job. The baseball writers admire Gehrig just as much as do the boys in the bleachers, and while, as honest reporters, they must write what they see and think, they do not like to do it. Their stories are tempered with their consideration for an aging, but still magnificent athlete.

"Whether or not Lou finally is reaching the end of his amazing career, there is no means of knowing at this range. There have been times in the past when it seemed he couldn't go on much longer, but somehow he always managed to rally at a critical point and go slugging on his way. There was a time no longer ago than last summer when he couldn't hit, couldn't run, and couldn't cover any ground around first base. In fact, he was so bad that a less patient, less understanding manager than Joe McCarthy would have hauled him out of the line-up. But Joe kept him in action and, as the end of the season drew on and the world series loomed, Lou was very like the Gehrig of old.

"Some time he is going to go, of course, and when he does, the chances are he will go overnight, like a great fighter who has been fighting for years and still *seems to be a great fighter until some night he gets in there with a strong young fellow who belts him out in a couple of rounds. Everybody is surprised until they look back and remember how long he has been fighting and how much punishment he has taken. Gehrig's unbroken string of ball games has imposed a terrific strain on him, but up to now Lou has been able to shake it off or bear up under it. But it is likely someday he will crash under it and crash so suddenly even those who are closest to him and know he hasn't much further to go will be surprised."*

The fellow who wrote that had read accurately between the lines of the stories filed out of St. Petersburg. Nobody, of course, knew what was wrong with Lou, but they thought he was through and were reluctant to come right out and say so.

The team broke camp and started north. Most of the time Lou looked no better than he had at Huggins Field or Waterfront Park, but the day before the Yankees and Dodgers, touring together as usual in the spring, jumped from Norfolk to Brooklyn, Lou made two home runs and two singles in four times at bat. To those who didn't see the game but merely read of it, the news was encouraging. It looked as if, with the opening of the season just a few days away, Lou was on the upswing.

And then the Yankees were home, playing the Dodgers at Ebbets Field. The day was gray and cold and the crowd was small, and in the dugout Mc-Carthy sat with his hands in the pockets of his windbreaker.

"How's DiMaggio?" a reporter who had not been with the team in the South asked. "How's Gordon? How's Ruffing? How's Gomez?"

"All right," McCarthy said. "All right. DiMaggio looks great. This is the first time we've had him through the whole training season. No accidents this time."

He tapped, for luck, on the wooden bench.

The reporter waited a moment. And then:

"How's Gehrig?"

McCarthy shook his head.

"I see he hit two home runs in Norfolk," the reporter said.

"He looked a little better there."

"Two home runs and two singles," the reporter said.

199

"The singles were all right," McCarthy said. "The home runs were fly balls over a short right-field fence."

The Yankees were going out for fielding practice.

"Watch Lou," McCarthy said.

Lou looked very bad. He would go down for a ground ball hit straight at him, and the ball would go through him. Or he would come up with the ball and throw it to second or third base and then start for first base to take a return throw, but he would be woefully slow. Back of first base, some fans jeered at him.

"Why don't you give yourself up?" one of them yelled. "What do you want McCarthy to do, burn that uniform off you?"

The reporter turned to McCarthy.

"He looks worse than I thought he would," he said "What's the matter with him, anyway?"

"I don't know."

"Is he through?"

McCarthy shrugged but said nothing.

"Are you going to open the season with him?"

"Yes."

The season opened. The Yankees played eight games. They were winning, but Lou was lagging. He made only four hits for an average of .143, and he was so slow covering first base that the other players had to wait for him before making a throw. Little was said about him in the newspapers but his team-mates were looking at him anxiously and the baseball writers talked about him among themselves. Nobody said anything to him about his poor playing, natur-ally. For one thing, he obviously was in a very bad mental state as he tried to pull himself together.

"How long can McCarthy keep him in there?" one writer asked another.

"I have an idea that when the Yankees go West, Joe will take him out. I think he just doesn't want to take him out while they are at home."

"And when he goes out . . . do you think it will be for good?"

"Maybe. Maybe if he just rests for a while, he will be all right."

The Yankees left for Detroit on the night of April 30. The next day was an off day. That day Lou spent alone, wrestling with the problem of his decline as a player, reaching a decision. McCarthy had spent the day at his home in Buffalo. When he reached Detroit on the morning of May 2, Lou was waiting for him in the lobby and went up to his room with him.

"Yes, Lou?" McCarthy said as the door of the room closed behind the boy who had carried his bags.

"I'm benching myself, Joe," Lou said.

McCarthy looked at him for a moment.

"Why?" he asked.

"For the good of the team," Lou said. "I can't tell you how grateful I am to you for the kindness you have shown me and for your patience. I've tried hard, Joe. You know that. But I just can't seem to get going, and nobody has to tell me how bad I've been and how much of a drawback I've been to the team. I've been thinking, ever since the season opened—when I saw that I couldn't start as I'd hoped I would—that the time had come for me to quit."

"Quit?" Joe said. "You don't have to quit. Take a rest for a week or so, and maybe you'll feel all right again."

Lou shook his head.

"I don't know," he said. "I don't know what's the matter with me. But I know I can't go on the way I am. . . . Johnny Murphy told me so."

McCarthy frowned angrily.

"Murphy told you! I'll—"

"No, Joe," Lou said. "I didn't mean it that way. All the boys have been so swell to me and nobody has said a word that would hurt my feelings. But Johnny Murphy said something the other day that made me know it was time for me to get out of the line-up. And all he meant to do was to be encouraging."

"How was that?"

"Do you remember the last play in the game—the last game at the Stadium?"

"Yes."

"A ball was hit between the box and first base—"

"And Johnny fielded it?"

"And I got back in time to take the throw—just in time?"

"Yes."

"I had a hard time getting back there, Joe," Lou said. "I should have been there in plenty of time. And then, as I made the put out and started for the clubhouse, Johnny waited for me near the box and said:

"'Nice play, Lou.'"

McCarthy was silent.

"I knew then that it was time to quit," Lou said. "When the boys were feeling sorry for me—"

"All right, Lou," Joe said. "Take a rest. I'll put Dahlgren on first base, but I want you to know that

203

that's your position—and whenever you want it back, all you have to do is to walk out there and take it."

The day had come. The day when he was to fulfill a promise he had made a year before. On an August day in 1938, he had come back to the dugout after taking a swing in batting practice and hadn't gone up again when it was his turn.

"What's the matter?" a reporter had asked.

"I have a bad thumb," he said. "I think maybe the darned thing is broken."

"Are you going to stay out of the line-up?"

"I should say not! It isn't as bad as that. I can grip a bat and handle the ball all right, and there is no reason why I shouldn't play."

"You aren't thinking too much about your record, are you?" the reporter asked.

"No," he said. "I'm all right. I can play. And I'll promise you this: When the day comes that I don't think I can help the ball club, I won't be in there, record or no record."

The day had come. The record had been set at 2,130 games.

There was, of course, no talk of him leaving the ball club. He still was captain of the Yankees, and every day there was a game he was in uniform, just as though he was going to play. And every day before the game he would take the batting order up to the umpires at the plate . . . and walk back to the dugout . . . and sit there and watch the game.

He had said once that when he no longer could play he would go fishing because he couldn't bear to sit and watch the Yankees play. But now he found he couldn't bear to go away—that, hard as it was for him to remain inactive as the game got under way, he couldn't leave the Yankees. They were on their way to another pennant, and he had to be there, even if he couldn't swing a bat to help them.

The other players tried to cheer him up.

"Quit jaking," they would say, "jaking" being the ball players' term for malingering. "Quit jaking and get in there and play ball."

And he would laugh and say:

"Next week."

One day, shortly after the Yankees had returned to the Stadium, he was sitting by a window in the clubhouse and Jake Powell and Vernon Gomez were clowning for his benefit. Powell hadn't been going too well himself, and Gomez was making fun of his own pitching efforts.

"Remember what a fast ball I used to have, Lou?" Gomez asked.

"I should say I do."

"Well, now when I throw it," Gomez said, "I could run up to the plate and catch it before it gets to the hitter."

"And if I was the hitter," Powell said, "you wouldn't have to worry about being cracked with the bat. I am so bad that if I swung at you as you ran across the plate I couldn't hit you."

Lou laughed and shook his head.

"I'd give a million dollars if I had a disposition like you two fellows," he said.

And after they had left him to go out to the field, he said:

"My friends tell me not to worry. They slap me on the back and say: 'Don't worry, Lou. Everything is going to be all right.' But how can I help worrying?"

When he had worried enough, he got into a plane and flew to the Mayo brothers' clinic at Rochester, Minnesota. He wanted to find out just what was the matter with him and when he reasonably could expect to play ball again.

The weather at Rochester was fine. He was in better spirits than he had been for some time. This, obviously, was the wise thing to do. Not to sit around and brood and wonder what was wrong. But to get to somebody who could tell him. If anything really was wrong with him, he could be treated for it, a cure quickly effected . . . and then he would be back on first base.

He was a smiling patient. Doctors, nurses, and clinic workers were attracted to him immediately, as every one was, wherever he went. Not because he was a great ball player but because he was such a fine and shy but friendly young man. A complete examination, the doctors said, would take a few days. There were certain tests to be made. That was perfectly agreeable to Lou.

"Take your time and give me the works," he said, laughing.

The tests began. The sports world waited, wondering what could be wrong with this still youthful giant who had captured its admiration by his feats on the ball field and its affection by—well, just by being the fellow he was.

The findings of the doctors shocked and bewildered not only the sport-minded but the whole nation. Their report was delivered to Ed Barrow by Lou on his return to New York. Signed by Dr. Harold C. Harbein, it read:

> "This is to certify that Mr. Lou Gehrig has been under examination at the Mayo Clinic from June 13 to June 19, 1939, inclusive.
>
> "After a careful and complete examination, it was found that he is suffering from amyotrophic lateral sclerosis. This type of illness involves the motor pathways and cells of the central nervous system and, in lay terms, is known as a form of chronic poliomyelitis —infantile paralysis.
>
> "The nature of this trouble makes it such that Mr. Gehrig will be unable to continue his active participation as a baseball player, inasmuch as it is advisable that he conserve his muscular energy. He could, however, continue in some executive capacity."

Few could pronounce the name of the disease, even fewer comprehend the nature of it. But it was, the doctors said, something like infantile paralysis. It was incredible that that fine, big body could harbor the frightful germ that robbed a man of his strength—of his life, perhaps.

Newspapers bombarded the Mayo Clinic with

208

questions. What did the report mean? How far had the disease progressed? Was there any relation between it and Lou's streak of consecutive games? Was there a cure for it? If so, what?

The doctors remained silent. They had made their report. They had nothing to add to it. Nor could further information be got from Lou. That was all he knew. It was all there in the report. They had told him to take it easy and had suggested the names of doctors in New York and in other towns where the Yankees played who could give him the treatment they had prescribed. In New Rochelle, Dr. M. W. Norton, who treated Lou when he was at his home in Larchmont, and who had known him for some time, naturally would not discuss the case.

The Yankee players were plunged in gloom.

"I knew there was something seriously wrong with him," Bill Dickey said. "I didn't know what it was, but I knew it was serious.

"We were in the room one day a few weeks ago," Bill said, "and Lou stumbled as he walked across the floor. I was reading a paper and looked up to see what he had stumbled over, but there was nothing there. I was going to ask him what had happened, but he had a strange look on his face and I didn't say anything. . . . A few days later he was standing looking out the window and I was sitting behind him, talking to him, and I saw one leg give way, just as though somebody had tapped him sharply at the back of the knee joint. He looked around, quick, to see if I had noticed it, I guess . . . but I didn't say anything.

"So I knew it was something serious," he said, and added, "but I didn't know it was as bad as this."

Ball players . . . fans . . . newspapermen . . . persons who had no interest in Lou as a ball player but whose sympathy had been aroused by his condition, asked themselves and each other just what the doctor's report actually meant.

In the study of his home in New Rochelle, Dr. Maurice Keady, who had no connection with the case, said to a friend:

"It is a death sentence. The prognosis is that he will live for from two to four years and that the end will come suddenly and painlessly."

How much did Lou know? Or guess? After his death, his wife, Eleanor, said:

"He never knew he was doomed. He thought, right up to the last few days, that he would get well."

"And you?"

210

"I knew it. I knew it within a few days after Lou came back from Rochester."

He never knew? Ah, but he did.

Shortly after he rejoined the team on his return from Rochester, the Yankees went to Washington for a series. As they got off the train and were walking down the platform, there was a trainload of Boy Scouts, on their way to or from a jamboree, on the next track, and the boys, catching sight of Lou, waved and shouted to him.

"Good luck!" they yelled. "Good luck, Lou!"

Lou was walking with Rud Rennie of the *Herald-Tribune*. He waved to the boys and smiled broadly, and then, turning to Rennie, he said:

"They're wishing me luck . . . and I'm dying."

And on the Fourth of July, which was Gehrig Appreciation Day at the Stadium, he sat in the dugout early in the afternoon as the stands were filling up and, indicating the right-field stand, where in the bright sunlight the fans were hurrying to their seats, he said to a reporter sitting next to him:

"It is going to be very hard to leave all this."

211

16. The Hall of Fame

GEHRIG Appreciation Day. A day set apart so that some of Lou's friends and admirers—after all, the Stadium will hold only about 80,000—could gather to pay tribute to him, to try to show him, however inadequately, how much they thought of him. The Fourth of July, and the Senators at the Stadium for a doubleheader, and, in the clubhouse, a calling up of old scenes in the minds of those who were of—or who closely had followed—the Yankees of 1927.

For there they were, some of them. Bob Meusel . . . Bob Shawkey . . . Herb Pennock . . . Waite Hoyt . . . Joe Dugan . . . Mark Koenig . . . Benny Bengough . . . Tony Lazzeri . . . Arthur Fletcher and Earle Combs, still, as coaches, wearing Yankee uniforms— and Gehrig, of course. And three Yankees of an even earlier vintage: Wally Schang, the best catcher the

Yankees ever had before the coming of Bill Dickey
. . . Wally Pipp, whose job Lou had taken in 1925
. . . and Everett Scott, whose record of playing
through 1,307 games had been smashed by Lou.

Most of them still looked very much as they had
when they were playing ball, although Scott had been
overtaken by the middle-age spread and somebody
said to him:

"Why, you are a little pappy guy now, Scottie!"

Scotty laughed as Lazzeri took a playful poke at his
bay window. The others looked as though they could
walk right out of that clubhouse and play a pretty
fair game of ball, and everybody laughed when Hoyt,
turning to the 1939 Yankees, said:

"Take those uniforms off and give them to us. We'll
handle the Senators for you."

And there were those who, looking on, remembered
the Fourth of July of 1927 and the Senators at the
Stadium and the Yankees slaughtering them in two
games and Joe Judge saying, as he left the park:

"I wish the season was over."

Least touched by the passing years was Meusel,
still slim and straight and silent as he was in the days
when he was trailing Ruth and Gehrig in the batting
order and hammering out home runs—or, on defense,

213

terrorizing enemy base-runners with the power that lay in his throwing arm.

They sat around and talked about the old days, and Lou sat with them and had them laughing with some of his stories, and the 1939 Yankees got up and went out, because there was work to be done on the field and also because they seemed to feel that they were intruding and that, for the moment at least, the clubhouse belonged to the heroes of 1927. So the old-timers sat there talking with Lou, and some reporters who had traveled with them sat there listening or telling stories themselves and Mark Roth, for many years the road secretary of the Yankees and still filling that post, stuck his head in the door and Meusel saw him and said:

"Hey! How about meal money for that jump from Detroit to Cleveland in 1927?"

Once in a while Gehrig or one of the others would look toward the door as though he was expecting somebody, which, as a matter of fact, everybody was: The Babe was missing. Lou was more than a little uneasy about the absence of the Babe. There had been stories of a coolness between him and the Babe and, as a matter of fact, there was truth in them. There was nothing serious behind this coolness. Simply that

214

in the last two or three years the old friendliness had worn thin. Things had been said, briefly, thought-lessly, on both sides. Lou, who once had taken the Babe's counsel so eagerly, had rejected it once or twice. On salary demands. On playing every day, even when he was handicapped by painful bruises. They saw each other infrequently and had little to say to each other.

But Lou didn't want that coolness to prevail today. This was his day, and he wanted the Babe there and the others in the clubhouse felt the Babe should be there. But it was nearly time for the first game and there was no sign of the Babe, and they went out, Lou and Fletcher and Combs to the dugout and the others to seats in boxes near the dugout.

McCarthy, deeply affected by Lou's illness, was nervous, almost irritable. He was afraid that the emotional strain would be too great for Lou and that it would give impetus to the progress of the disease. Ceremonies had been arranged, to take place between games, and Joe knew he would have to speak over the public-address system to the crowd, and he dreaded it. And Lou, in the dugout, was nervous now. He looked around the edge of the dugout to where Eleanor sat with his mother and father and

215

Mrs. Barrow and Mrs. McCarthy, and they smiled at him and he smiled back and felt a little better.

"He was worrying about his speech," Eleanor said later. "He was composing it at home last night and he kept crossing out sentences and rewriting them, and finally I said to him:

" 'Let me see if I can't help you.'

"And he said: 'No, thanks, Eleanor. Not this time. This must be my speech and I must say these things my way.' "

Now the game started—with George Pipgras, another 1927 Yankee, as one of the umpires—and the Yankees were winning, but it was not a particularly exciting game. And then, suddenly, there was a roar from the crowd and fans were standing up and craning their necks to see what it was all about, and there was the Babe coming in with Mrs. Ruth and waving to the crowd as they made their way toward their seats in the boxes with the other 1927 players. The Yankees in the dugout stuck their heads out to see the cause of the excitement and when Lou saw the Babe he was happy.

When the first game was over, a microphone was set up at the plate and the players of both teams and the Yankees of 1927 and baseball writers and club

and league officials gathered about. And Mayor Fio-
rello H. LaGuardia of New York and James A. Farley, then Postmaster General of the United States.
And as the Babe came striding to the plate, he threw
his arms around Lou and hugged him tight, and Lou
was so happy he didn't know whether to laugh or cry.

Sid Mercer, dean of the baseball writers in New
York, was the master of ceremonies. First there was
the presentation of gifts. From the Yankees. From
the Giants. From the Stevens family. From the Babe.
From the baseball writers. From the employees of
the club—ushers and ticket-sellers, clerks and gate-
men and ground keepers. And then the speeches,
with the crowd silent, intent upon catching every
word. LaGuardia . . . Farley . . . McCarthy. Joe's
voice broke almost as he began to talk. And then,
almost hysterically, he said:

"But don't let us cry about this . . ."

And very nearly did.

At last it was Lou's turn. The speech he had prepared the night before had been discarded.

"They say I have had a bad break," he said. "But
when the office force and the ground keepers and
even the Giants from across the river, whom we'd
give our right arm to beat in the world series—when

they remember you, that's something. . . . And when you have a wonderful father and mother who worked hard to give you an education . . . and a wonderful wife . . ."

His voice was trailing off. In the stands it was difficult to hear what he was saying.

"And there is one man who, I wish, could be with us here today but he . . ."

"He's talking of Colonel Ruppert," somebody in the press box said.

Ruppert had died in January of that year.

" . . . and Miller Huggins . . . and Joe McCarthy . . . and Ed Barrow. When you have the privilege of rooming with and knowing one of the finest fellows that ever lived, Bill Dickey . . ."

There were tears in his eyes now and in his voice. And then:

"I may have been given a bad break, but I have an awful lot to live for. With all this, I consider myself the luckiest man on the face of this earth."

The crowd, greatly moved, sat silent for a moment as Lou stepped back from the microphone, brushing the tears across his cheeks. And then the crowd roared its homage to him. And in the press box, somebody said:

"I have written about a lot of game guys in my

time. But there goes the gamest guy of them all."

For Lou was walking now . . . and the crowd saw with sadness that his step already was faltering . . . toward the dugout. All the gifts but one were being carried by attendants. He carried the one he prized most. This was a silver trophy, presented to him by his teammates, and on a bronze plate at the base of it was inscribed a poem, "To Lou Gehrig," written by John Kieran at the request of the players:

We've been to the wars together;
We took our foes as they came;
And always you were the leader,
And ever you played the game.
Idol of cheering millions;
Records are yours by sheaves;
Iron of frame they hailed you,
Decked you with laurel leaves.
But higher than that we hold you,
We who have known you best;
Knowing the way you came through
Every human test.
Let this be a silent token
Of lasting friendship's gleam
And all that we've left unspoken.
         —Your pals of the Yankee team.

The last line was in script and led into the signatures of all the players.

It was shortly after this that Lou was elected to Baseball's Hall of Fame at Cooperstown, N. Y. This shrine of baseball's immortals stands near the field where, in 1839—or so the baseball authorities are satisfied after exhaustive research and in the face of heated claims on behalf of other men and other towns —Abner Doubleday and Alexander Cartwright conceived the sport and organized the first teams.

The field, reclaimed from the weeds that had grown about it through years of neglect, and converted into a modern ball park, and the Hall of Fame, made possible by funds subscribed in Cooperstown, were dedicated in 1939 on a day given over to the one hundredth anniversary of baseball and marked also by a game between two teams of major league stars. In the Hall are busts of the mighty. Of Grover Cleveland Alexander and John McGraw . . . of Ty Cobb and Tris Speaker . . . of Walter Johnson and Willie Keeler and Napoleon Lajoie . . . of Hans Wagner and Cy Young and Eddie Collins and Christy Mathewson and Connie Mack . . . of Babe Ruth and

George Sisler . . . and of Buck Ewing and Cap Anson and Charlie Comiskey and Old Horse Radbourne and A. G. Spaulding and George Wright and Arthur Cummings . . . and of Doubleday and Cartwright, whose genius had made it possible.

And now there had been a great surge of public sentiment for the election of Lou to this company of men who had laid the foundations of baseball or had built upon them so well. He was eligible because his career had ended—prematurely and pathetically, but definitely ended. And he belonged with the other greats for he, too, had contributed not only to the brilliance of baseball but to its soundness and honesty and decency as well.

There was a quick response to the public sentiment. He was unanimously elected.

This moved him greatly. It seemed incredible to him that it had happened. That from his humble beginning as a ball player on the sandlots of New York he had achieved a fame as enduring as that of baseball itself and that in years to come, small boys would see his likeness and his records in that building, colonial in design. And that, as they walked the streets of the lovely town on the shore of Lake Otsego ("If baseball wasn't actually cradled here, it should have

221

been," somebody had said on dedication day), they might speak of him and the things he did.

Some of the other names in the Hall of Fame had appeared in the same box scores with his. Alexander and Sisler and Speaker and Cobb and the Babe and Collins and Johnson. As a kid, he had read about . . . and idolized . . . Wagner and Keeler and Lajoie and Young. Some of the others were but names to him and, it must be confessed, had made but vague imprints on his mind. Connie Mack he knew well and admired tremendously, though all his years in the major leagues had been devoted in part to beating the teams that Connie managed. McGraw had . . . well . . . frightened him when he was a kid just off the Columbia campus. But he had got to know McGraw in later years—to know him and to like him. And more than once McGraw, looking at him and smiling and shaking his head, had said:

"I wish I had paid more attention to you when you were on the Polo Grounds."

And now he was one of that illustrious crew. One with Cobb, who, they said, was the greatest of all ball players—although Lou would dispute that hotly, claiming the Babe was the greatest—one with Johnson . . . and Matty . . . and Alexander . . . with Lajoie and Collins, rivals for the distinction of having been the greatest second-baseman, with Willie Keeler, whose prescription for getting base hits ("I hit 'em where they ain't") had become part of baseball's traditions, with Wagner, undoubtedly the greatest of all short stops and, according to McGraw and Ed Barrow, the greatest of all players, including Ruth and Cobb.

Lou set great store by the honors that he reaped from the baseball field. Sure, he was a professional and he was well paid for his ball playing. His ball playing made him a moderately rich man, and he liked that, too, not for the money itself but for the things money would buy—the things that it enabled him to do for his mother and father and for Eleanor. But he was grateful for the stories that were written about him in the newspapers, for the things that were said about him on the radio, for the countless letters he received from people all over the country—especially in that summer of 1939, when the gravity of his illness became known—and for the other forms of recognition accorded him because of his skill.

And this, in some respects, was the greatest that ever had come to him. For it placed him among the half-gods of baseball.

The season rolled on. So did the Yankees. Once
. . . in the first two weeks of the season, they had
been as low as third place. They were to sink that
low again in May, but that was all. On May 11 they
swung into first place, and from there on it was a
foregone conclusion that they would win, which they
did by a margin of seventeen games over the Red
Sox.

Lou was as happy that summer as he possibly
could have been under the circumstances. He never
could play ball again but in his attendance at the
ball park he was as faithful as he had been when he
was making his remarkable record. His presence in
the dougout was a source of inspiration and encouragement to the other players and, somewhat to
his surprise, he found an unsuspected joy in watching
the games—he who once had thought it would be
impossible for him to remain idle as the Yankees
played.

"Do you know," he said one day at the Stadium,
"I am getting a terrific kick out of watching Crosetti
and Gordon at work about second base."

"You talk as if you hadn't seen those boys before,"
Combs said.

"Well, in one way, I saw very little of them when

I was playing," Lou said. "That may sound funny but it's true."

"How come?"

"Because every time they were handling the ball I was on my way to cover first base and I never got a good look at them."

"And now that you are getting a good look at them you think—"

"I think they're pretty good," Lou said, grinning.

And then he said:

"You'd be surprised how different a slant you get on a ball game when you see it from the bench—I mean, after you have been playing for years. For the first time, I am looking at a complete game. For years I was so busy trying to take care of my own position that I didn't have time to take in a view of the whole game."

They were wise, the doctors at the Mayo Clinic, who counseled him to remain with the team. Sitting in the dugout . . . lounging in the clubhouse . . . talking with the other players and the baseball writers . . . moving from town to town . . . took his mind off his illness through most of his waking hours. And the thrill of another pennant fight, vicarious though it was this time, surged within him as the

Yankees, at home or roaming the hostile towns, drove back and flattened the enemy.

The players kept alive the old gag about Lou "jaking," pretending that if he really wanted to play he could do so and that he merely was taking the easy way out, getting into the park for nothing and riding around the country and enjoying himself—also for nothing. Lou never seemed to tire of the gag, either. And yet there was a day—

It was before a game at the Stadium, and George Selkirk came up the steps from the clubhouse and picked a bat out of the tray in front of the dugout and started for the plate to hit a few in batting practice.

"Get hot, George," Lou said. "I want to see you hit a couple into the stand today."

Selkirk turned and looked at him steadily for a moment and then he said:

"What are you telling me what to do for? If you had any guts, you'd get in there and hit a couple yourself."

A smile flicked at Gehrig's lips and then vanished.

"I wish to God I could, George," he said.

But save in moments like that he was at least outwardly happy, talking to his teammates, yelling to the players on the opposing clubs, kidding the umpires. He still roomed with Dickey, of course, when the club was on the road, and they ate together and, at night, would join with other players or newspapermen in a card game. Or they would go to an early movie and then back to their room, and Lou would read or listen to Bill talk about hunting in Arkansas in the late fall when the leaves are brown and the quail whir through the air as the dogs flush them.

Once Bill was talking about hunting as he sat in a hotel lobby with Lou and some of the other players, and one of them said:

"Lou, why don't you go hunting with Bill in the fall?"

"Him hunt!" Bill exclaimed. "He couldn't shoot a bird, or anything else, the big sissy."

"Is that right?" the other player asked.

Lou nodded.

"Is it right?" Bill said. "Of course, it's right. I was telling him one day about quail hunting and he told me the only time he ever killed a bird was when he was a kid. He hit it with a bean shooter and when he saw he had killed it, he felt so bad he cried and dug a hole for the bird in the back yard and buried it. He'd be a fine guy to take hunting, wouldn't he?"

The Reds won the pennant in the National League in 1939, and the Yankees beat them in what had come to be regarded as the usual Yankee fashion— four games in a row. The crowds in Cincinnati cheered Lou, as did the crowds in the American League cities during the season . . . and watched, with pity in their eyes, as he shuffled up and down the dugout steps or, where a long flight of stairs had to be negotiated, how he clung to the banister for support.

The series ended in Cincinnati and the Yankees were on their way back to New York on a special train, and shortly after dinner there was a party in McCarthy's drawing room. Eleanor Gehrig was there and she seemed rather uneasy, and Mrs. Barrow said to her:

"What's the matter?"

"I was just wondering about Lou," Eleanor said.

"Where he is?"

"That's what I was wondering."

"Well," Mrs. Barrow said, smiling, "I'm sure he can't be far off."

Eleanor got up and went out. In a few minutes she was back, smiling.

"He's all right," she said. "He is playing bridge

228

with Bill Dickey, John Kieran, and Grant Rice."

"And now will you sit still and enjoy yourself?" somebody asked.

"Yes," she said. "For a little while. Lou has to get to bed early, you know."

It was Lou's last train ride. He couldn't have known that then, but he did know it was his last with the Yankees. And then he would be at the Stadium in the morning with the other players, who would be clearing their lockers in the clubhouse of their personal belongings. And for the last time he would be taking his stuff out of his locker, and Fred Logan, the clubhouse man who has been with the Yankees ever since the old days on the hilltop when the team was known as the Highlanders, would be taking his uniform from him.

And Number Four, which had been Lou's number since he joined the team would be retired so that, in years to come, no player ever would wear it. And Ed Barrow had told him that his connection with the ball club would not be severed but the Yankees would carry him on their rolls as a voluntarily retired player—voluntarily retired players remaining, in theory under baseball law, the property of the club with which they last played.

Wonder if, on that last train ride, he thought of his first? Of the night, back in 1920, when, as a member of the High School of Commerce team, he lay in the darkness of his berth and the train rushed on toward Chicago?

17. The Parole Board

IF, when the last echo of the world series had died away and Lou was at home in Larchmont, he pondered what he was going to do to occupy his time, he didn't have to ponder long. On October 10th the telephone rang. Mayor LaGuardia, a voice said, wanted to speak to Lou.

"Hello, Mr. Mayor! How are you?"

"Fine, Lou, thanks. And you?"

"Great, Mr. Mayor. I'm feeling fine, really. The next time I go to Mayo Brothers for a check-up, those doctors are going to be surprised."

"Well, that's fine. Fine. . . . Lou, what are you going to do, now that you're out of a job? We can't have young fellows like you hanging around doing nothing, you know."

"Why, I haven't quite decided. I have a number of things in mind and I—"

"I have something in mind for you, myself," the

231

Mayor said. "I believe you are just the man for the job, and I know you will get a kick out of it. At least, I hope you will. It means an opportunity to serve a lot of young fellows who haven't had much of a break from life and could stand a lot of help."

"That sounds great," Lou said. "What is it?"

"A position on the New York City Parole Board. There is a vacancy on the Board, and you're my first choice for the job because you can do a great deal, especially for the youngsters that have been caught up by the law. How does it sound to you?"

"Why, I think it's wonderful! But are you sure I can handle it? After all, I've had no experience in anything like this and I—"

"You don't need experience as much as you do the kind of mind and heart you have," the Mayor said. "There's only one thing more you need to qualify."

"What's that?"

"You live in Larchmont now?"

"Yes."

"Move to New York. The law says that the appointee must be a resident of New York City. . . . Well, what do you say?"

"Why, yes, of course, Mr. Mayor. By all means. I am delighted."

232

"Good," the Mayor said. "I'll make the appointment right now and announce it to the newspapers. And we're delighted to have you."

"Thank you, Mr. Mayor. Thank you."

"All right, Lou. Good-by—oh, hold on a minute!"

"Yes, sir. I'm still on."

"I forgot to tell you the salary. It's six thousand dollars a year. Is that satisfactory?"

"Satisfactory? Why, I didn't know any salary went with it."

"Well, it does. Now, good luck to you, Lou—and good househunting."

Eleanor was as pleased as Lou. She knew something of social service and saw in the position a great opportunity for a man of Lou's qualities to help countless youngsters who, many times solely as a result of environment, had got on the wrong road. She knew they would look up to Lou and be more responsive to his influence than they would to that of almost anyone else.

They set out the next day to find a house in New York. Not too far downtown, for they liked the trees and flowers and the bright morning sun in the suburbs. They found, after a day or so, the house they had in mind. A snug, two-story red brick house just off the Henry Hudson Parkway—and just safely within the northern boundary of New York.

"Like it, Lou?" she asked.

"I think it's swell."

"We'll put the piano here," she said, standing in the living room, "and the couch over there and—"

She looked into the library, just beyond the living room.

"You know what that's going to be, don't you?" she asked.

"The library?"

"Yes, but your trophy room as well. Now we have a room in which we can put all the trophies you have collected. We won't have to put them in odd corners or hide them in closets. That one the boys gave you can stand right there opposite the door, so that a person entering the room will see it first of all. And those valuable player trophies from the Sporting News will go over there—and on this wall I am going to hang that picture of you. And—oh, Lou, I hardly can wait to move in, so that we can have the things just the way we want them. It will look lovely."

It did, too. The sunken dining room . . . the wide living room with its open fireplace . . . the trophy room . . . the shining kitchen . . . upstairs the bedrooms and "the office," as they called it, a square room, its walls hung with baseball pictures and a desk in one corner where Eleanor could write or Lou could sit as he studied the cases that came before him on the Parole Board.

He had plunged into this new work as eagerly and as enthusiastically as he had plunged into baseball as a boy. His work day didn't begin when he went to the office of the Board in the morning, nor end when he left it at night. He brought records and testimony home with him and studied them at night and, very often, again in the morning before Eleanor drove him downtown.

His appointment had been a very happy choice on LaGuardia's part and was hailed as such by public-spirited citizens and in the editorial columns of the newspapers. Lou might have been a grand person for the job if he had been no more than just the former first-baseman of the Yankees, because kids and young fellows look up to major league ball players, especially great ball players, and there have been few, even among the great ones, who have ranked close to him over a fourteen-year span.

But in Gehrig's case it went much deeper than that. Lou was born and brought up in New York. He played on the streets and he was chased by the cops (and once even arrested, remember?), and he ran with kids who wound up in Sing Sing. Some of them were good kids, too, when they started. But they hit the wrong lane and followed it until they got into serious trouble. And maybe, somewhere along the way, somebody could have taken them by the arm and steered them right and they would have wound up as useful citizens.

He meant to give the young fellows who came before him all the thought and all the consideration he could—to be, if possible, the one who could check them in time and show them the right way to live. And since he was such an appealing figure and, besides, could talk the young fellows' language, he was successful, and there is many a young man in New York today who is doing well because he got a break from Lou.

Meanwhile, in his leisure time, Lou was pursuing a love of music instilled in him by his mother and father and nurtured quietly through the years— quietly because he feared that if he talked about it his teammates would laugh at him and the newspapermen would think he was putting on airs—and developed by Eleanor. Music had been the foremost interest in her life until she met Lou. She studied it, played it, composed songs, several of which had been published. Unexpectedly, she found in her husband an eager pupil, and she taught him eagerly.

They attended concerts or the opera, or on nights at home she played for him or talked to him of music and the men and women who had written or interpreted it.

"He used to say to me once in a while," she said, afterward, " 'I wonder what the boys would say if they could see me now.' "

"Now" would be a night at Carnegie Hall or the Metropolitan. Or, perhaps, a night in the house in Riverdale, Lou sitting in his big chair before the fireplace and Eleanor playing the piano . . . or sitting close to him as they listened to a recording of a symphony.

Or there would be drives through the pleasant Westchester countryside or the rolling Connecticut hills and dinner with friends. Or dinner in town and the theater. Or a night at home, with Mom and Pop for dinner or Ed and Mrs. Barrow. Or John and Alma Kieran and Joe and Josephine Stevens.

No one ever had a more pleasant home. No one, released from the hubbub and tumult of the baseball wars, ever had a more restful haven. . . . Yet over it a shadow lengthened and deepened.

So passed the fall and winter. With the coming of late February, the ball clubs were beginning to head south once more. For the first time since 1924 when, virtually penniless, he had gone to New Orleans, Lou wasn't going south. Somebody wrote a line about that in one of the newspapers. Somebody else, reading it, wondered how Lou felt and dropped in at the Parole Board office.

To his surprise, he found that Lou had become completely reconciled to the fact that he never again would sink his spikes into the turf of Huggins Field nor hit a ball into the trees on the rim of the park. He was smiling, cheerful . . . and completely engrossed in his work.

"Sure, I'd like to be going south with the Yankees," he said. "And so, I guess, would about a million other fellows. But I'm luckier than they are—because I've been south with the Yankees. I had a long stretch in baseball, and I enjoyed every minute of it. Now that's behind me, and I have this work to do."

His glance swept the top of his big desk, littered and piled with books and papers.

"This is important work, too," he said, soberly. "I have a great responsibility because I am dealing with the lives of young men—many of them little more than boys."

And then:

"Of course, I'll read every word that comes out of St. Petersburg and the other training camps," he said. "Think the Yankees can win again?"

The visitor shrugged.

"Possibly," he said. "Although five pennants in a row would be something unheard of. It nearly happened once, though."

"When was that?" Lou asked.

"When the Athletics won in 1910 and 1911 and, having lost out to the Red Sox in 1912, came back to win in 1913 and 1914. I say it nearly happened because Connie Mack says that the 1912 team was the strongest of all and but for some very bad breaks would have won."

"Well," Lou said, "if any team can do it, we can. Nobody ever had a finer or more spirited bunch of players than we have, and certainly we have the best manager in baseball today and one of the best that ever lived."

Note the "we." He never considered himself as

239

anything but a member of the Yankees. He no longer could play, but they still were his team. In spirit, he still was one of them.

Six weeks later the teams came north, the season started. Lou's once powerful body was wasting perceptibly, his feet dragged as he walked. Yet his spirits remained high and his interest in the Yankees keen. When the good weather came on, he was a frequent visitor at the Stadium. He would sit in the clubhouse with McCarthy and the players and sometimes drop into the visiting players' clubhouse to see his friends on the other teams. And then, although it had become a torturous journey for him, he would go down the steep flight of stairs and under the stand to the dugout and sit there before the game, watching the batting practice. When the game began he would sit in a box close to the dugout. If it was a one-sided game, he would leave before it was over so that he would not be caught in the rush of the fans for the exits, but if it was a close game, he stuck to the finish. He couldn't leave the Yankees until they had won—or lost—a close one.

A great friend to him at this time was Ed Barrow. Barrow had been his friend from that day back in June of 1923 when he had walked into the Yankees' office with Andy Coakley to confer with Barrow and Paul Krichell about signing a contract. In all the years that followed, he reached his agreements on contracts with Barrow, went to him often for advice on personal matters, and rightly regarded him as one on whom he could depend at any time.

He respected Colonel Ruppert for what he was and admired him for the things he had done in baseball, but he never felt close to the Colonel, as the Babe did, for instance. The Babe called the Colonel "Jake" and never signed a contract without talking it over with him. Lou never talked business with him, always was shy in his presence, and probably never had more than a five-minute conversation with him at any one time.

And now, with his baseball days behind him and new problems rising before him, there was even an added warmth in his friendship for Barrow. They visited each other's homes and Lou would see Ed at the ball park or drop into the office on Forty-second Street, and they had long talks together that were stimulating to Lou. And Mom and Pop and Eleanor were fond of big Ed, with his shaggy eyebrows and gruff manner, so that he was looked upon as one of the family.

241

The summer waned. So did Lou's hopes of seeing his team win the pennant for the fifth time in a row. McCarthy did a magnificent job as he held the team together, keeping it from cracking as key players stumbled and faltered, but although they put on a fine late season drive and were in the race right up to the last week or so of the season, they couldn't quite get up there. They were so close, as the season rushed to its end, that if they had had Gehrig in the full flush of his vigor on first base, they could have won. But Gehrig could only look on now.

The pennant went to the Detroit Tigers, and the Reds won in the National League and there was no world series in New York for the first time since 1936. The Yankees scattered for the winter, to go hunting or fishing or to play golf or farm, and Lou said good-by to them and went back to his desk in the Parole Board office and the snug house off the Henry Hudson Parkway.

And now another winter came on. As it closed in about them, the Gehrigs went out less and less. Days at the office, even when the press of cases before him was light, were fatiguing for Lou. It had been some time since he could drive his car (with its license plate L G 1 that every traffic cop knew and saluted as it passed), but Eleanor was there every evening to pick him up. They would drive home to dinner, sometimes having guests in, much more often just the two of them sitting at the candle-lit table, for Lou had to retire early.

John Kieran, whose home is near by, would drop in of an evening to talk of sports or music or literature or nature and, once in a while, bring his accordion and play for Lou and Eleanor. Or Pitzy Katz, who although a successful businessman in New York has few rivals even among the professionals as an imitator and dialectician, and he would have them howling with his stories. Other friends would call, Ed Barrow more frequently than any save Kieran and Katz. And the telephone would ring and there would be friends calling to ask how Lou was and if they might drop in some time, and Eleanor would say:

"We'd love to have you. Come any time, because we don't go out much any more and Lou is so glad to see his friends. But—and I hate to do this—I must ask you not to stay late. He would sit up here all night talking if I would let him, but he must have his rest."

And, of course, Mom and Pop, who were living in Mt. Vernon, would drive over regularly, and they would talk about Lou's boyhood and the days when he was just a young fellow with the Yankees.

A pleasant life still. But the tempo of it grew slower . . . and slower.

18. The Last Days

ANOTHER spring . . . the ball season on again . . . and now Lou rapidly was growing weaker. There were days when, although he got up in the morning, he didn't feel like going to his office, and Eleanor would call up and say he wouldn't be in that day. And Lou would read or pore over the papers on his desk upstairs in the square room they called the office. Or play the phonograph . . . or sit by the window, looking out toward the parkway . . . and thinking . . . of what?

Of baseball, probably. For now, slowed down to a halting walk, tiring after the least exertion, unable to go regularly to his office in town, it is likely that his mind dwelt frequently on baseball. For baseball had been so very much a part of his life that it had seemed, at one time, almost to be his life itself.

All that he had had sprung from baseball. The

tangible things. The security he had provided for his mother and father, the homes in which they had lived in New Rochelle and Larchmont, his boat on the Sound, his fishing tackle, his car. Those trips he had taken to the Orient and around the world. Those trophies in the library. His niche in the Hall of Fame.

And the intangible things. The love of Eleanor, whom he never would have met if he hadn't been a ball player. The memories of their years together. Of sunny days on the Florida keys and frost-bite days on the Sound. Memories of the days when he was storming the American League towns with the Yankees or playing in a packed Stadium at home. . . . Of games won and lost . . . and world series . . . and trains whistling through the night.

Of the friendships he had made and cherished and of how much it had meant to him to know Ed Barrow and little Miller Huggins and Joe McCarthy and the Babe and Benny Bengough and Christy Walsh . . . and Bill Dickey.

There had been little else in his life but baseball, and most of that little had sprung directly from baseball. Christy Walsh had syndicated newspaper articles under his name, had arranged for him to sell his endorsements of bats, gloves, caps, and breakfast foods, even had made a motion picture star of him once. A recollection of that always made Lou smile. "Rawhide," the picture was called. It was the story of a city-bred cowboy and it was very bad indeed, and Lou knew that as well as anybody and it was at once the beginning and the end of his motion picture career. Once, too, he had embarked on an off-season venture as a customer's man for a brokerage firm but he was no more a customer's man than he was an actor, and he knew that, too.

The air was soft. There were blossoms on the trees and the shrubs were green and there were flowers about the doorway. In a few days it would be June. Wonder if, as he looked back across the years, he realized what a fateful month June had been in his life? He was born on June 19, 1903. As a schoolboy he had hit that home run at Wrigley Field in June of 1920. In June of 1923 he joined the Yankees and saw his name in a major league box score for the first time. On June 1, 1925, he had begun his streak of consecutive games, and on June 2, 1925, he had become the regular first-baseman. On June 3, 1932, he had hit four home runs in a game in Philadelphia. And now, in a few days, it would be June again. . . .

Eleanor didn't know that he knew he was doomed. But he did. And she never let him know she knew their days together were numbered and that the numbers were dropping fast.

"There," the fellow in the press box had said that Fourth of July at the Stadium, "goes the gamest guy I ever saw."

The gamest guy had found a mate as game as he.

On the night of June 2, there was a sudden change in his condition. What Eleanor first thought was drowsiness after a day propped against the pillows on his bed reading and listening to the radio was, she quickly realized, a coma.

The doctor was at the house in a few minutes. Mom and Pop, shaken and frightened, were driving over from Mt. Vernon. Ed Barrow, roused from an easy chair in his home in Larchmont, was being whirled across the parkways by a driver who, that night, gave no thought to speed cops.

Shortly before ten o'clock, Lou opened his eyes and looked at those grouped about the bed. He seemed surprised to see them there, for they had not been there just a . . . a . . . moment before. And then, as though he had fallen asleep again, he died.

Death had brought no pain. Only bewilderment.

In newspaper offices and radio stations across the country, the report of his death came as a shock, as it did when it was announced to the public. Within an hour, messages of sympathy were pouring in on the bereaved parents and widow, and cars lined the streets about the house. The Babe and Mrs. Ruth arrived in tears.

In Detroit, Joe McCarthy stepped out of a taxicab in front of the hotel where the Yankees were staying and the manager of the hotel said to him:

"Gehrig died tonight."

Joe was shaken as though he had been struck in the face and as he walked into the lobby and saw some of the players gathered there, he saw that they knew, for they were gray and stunned. And in his room, that he had shared so long with Lou, Bill Dickey cried.

By order of Mayor LaGuardia, flags flew at half-staff in New York the next day, as the city, and the nation, mourned the death of this young man. Thousands of persons filed past his bier as he lay in state in a little church in Riverdale. The newspapers carried editorials citing his gallantry and deploring his untimely death. From the White House, from the

Governor's mansion at Albany, from the homes of children who played on the sidewalks as he once had done, came expressions of grief.

He died as he had lived. Bravely, quietly. To his mother, to his wife, to all who knew and loved him, to the millions who sorrowed at his death, he left the shining legacy of courage.